If You Love Your Family, Save Like It

If You Love Your Family, Save Like It

Money Management for Modern America

NICOLE PETERKIN

NEXT CENTURY
PUBLISHING

If You Love Your Family, Save Like It

Published by Next Century Publishing
Austin, TX
www.NextCenturyPublishing.com

ISBN: 978-1-68102-109-6

Printed in the United States of America

For Daddy, who taught me everything

CONTENTS

If You Love
Your Family,
Save Like It

ACKNOWLEDGMENTS

First of all, I would like to thank my sister, Melissa Peterkin, who constantly challenges my views and beliefs and pushes me to see the other side of the story. Thank you for being my constant sounding board and always supporting me even when you don't agree with my opinions. I appreciate your understanding that I wrote this book with good intentions. I couldn't have gotten clear on exactly what I believe and why I believe it so strongly without you playing devil's advocate.

To the rest of my family, who have always trusted in my ability to just do it, I appreciate you. Mom, Chris, Matt, Greg—I love you guys.

My gratitude goes out to everyone who went through this book-birthing process alongside me.

I would also like to thank all those without whose love, friendship, and lessons I wouldn't be who I am today, including Stacy Doherty, Will Bett, Rielle Grant, Melissa Par, and Alyssa Trinidad. You've lived life with me through the good and the bad: learning together, working together, sharing stories, growing together, and helping to shape the way I look at the world. I couldn't have written this without your love and support.

PREFACE

"You can always count on Americans to do the right thing - after they've tried everything else."
—Winston Churchill

The vast majority of Americans don't love their families.

I know this because to love your family, you need to act like you do instead of just saying you do.

For many parents, love means never saying no. It means opening up the wallet at every opportunity when their kids ask. Yes to expensive vacations and cars funded on credit. Yes to designer clothes for the first day of school. Yes to sky-rocketing tuition, without a plan to pay it back.

The actions of many Americans simply aren't very loving when you look at the consequences. Millions of us carry massive credit card debt, have minimal savings, and are relying on Social Security alone for retirement income. If you love your family, you need to handle your money in a way that proves it.

We all say aloud that we are going to help our kids pay for their education and save diligently so we can enjoy a long and enjoyable life. But how many of us put off figuring out to how make these goals a reality? How many of us are banking on hope instead of making a real plan for financial independence?

Instead of determining that you need to save an additional $500 per month in order to retire on time, or planning so your son or daughter won't need to take out student loans, or looking for ways to cut back and ways to create leverage with your money, we say we're too busy or too scared to know the reality. Or worse, we finally work with someone who tells us what's needed to reach our goals - and then we continue doing the same thing we've always done instead of making changes. We refuse to change because different actions, loving actions, might mean giving up those "luxuries" we regularly spend thousands of dollars on without thinking twice about; things like premium cable and unlimited cell phone plans.

Many of us avoid making plans for our money because we know that this process will involve correcting bad money habits, taking a hard look at some lifestyle choices, and deciding what is most important to us. These are tough questions for any of us to consider. But not making a plan doesn't save us from the eventual repercussions of these choices; it just means being blindsided and potentially worse off when that time comes.

I get it! Saving money can be very hard. Changing habits is hard. Decision-making is hard. But you know what else is hard? Being broke. Being a victim of your situation when life happens because you didn't plan. Not having the money to be able to take advantage of the best opportunities when they present themselves, during both hard times and good times. Always being behind the eight-ball when it comes to your finances.

I know—it's not your fault that you didn't start off on the right footing when it comes to your finances. No one taught you how to plan and save and manage your money. Your parents didn't talk about it. Your teachers didn't have curriculum around it. And you're busy. You work hard, and when you're done you want to spend time with those who matter. You don't have time to sift through all of the conflicting financial advice out there, and hiring someone is not in your budget because you don't have a budget.

Trust me—I get it! But I also get that if you choose not to make a change now and continue making excuses and placing blame instead of writing a different story, your financial situation becomes your fault and your excuses will end up costing you thousands of dollars. If you don't take personal responsibility for your financial situation and change your actions from here on out, guess what's going to happen? You will suffer. But even worse, your family—the people you love—will suffer. At some point, your parents, siblings, and kids will all have to deal with the repercussions of your decisions; either directly, indirectly, or both. You've seen it happen to other people, and might have even experienced it yourself. So why are you going to continue down the same path and let that happen to you?

I grew up watching my dad sacrifice time with us for more money. The truth is that he didn't properly leverage his resources to get back his time and he didn't have a proper financial plan. My grandmother taught him that hard work, a strong work ethic, and education were the keys to success and that mastering those fundamentals would allow him to give his family the best of everything. My dad taught us those very same fundamentals, and I began to follow in his footsteps at an early age; getting my first job at 16 and working multiple jobs, always striving to be the best in every position, strategically working my way up to earn more and improve my titles. Like him, I sacrificed time with my family for more money, more hours, and more independence, with the end goal of corporate success.

When my dad died suddenly at 47, I realized that our family had truly been robbed. My dad was a chemical engineer who had climbed the corporate ladder time and time again. He had a multi-six-figure income and a prestigious title to show for it. We'd been given everything we needed and much of what we wanted. He was even able to financially help his siblings as well. But the cost of that lifestyle was time and memories with him. Looking at the pieces of his financial picture after he was gone, I realized it didn't have to be that way.

My dad was a saver, that's for sure. However, he saved by default according to the conventional wisdom rather than by a personalized plan for our family. With some guidance and a thorough plan, my dad could've done more with what he had. He could have used his resources differently to still provide for the future while having the best possible lifestyle in the present, including spending more time as a family. It's not that my dad spent every minute working. He worked a regular 40-hour work week and he worked hard at his job, but when he came home he had to continue to "work" on our finances. Instead of working with someone knowledgeable to come up with a plan so that he could spend just a little bit of time and energy working the plan, he'd come home and sit at the computer looking at his investments and trying to figure out the best way to pay all the bills, keep our lifestyle, and send his four kids to college. He was always worrying and wondering and obsessing over the numbers and how to best maneuver them.

Instead he could have had a roadmap and, knowing his plan was taken care of, been able to spend more time with us. Seeing this so clearly, I used what I learned from his mistakes to invest in real estate and build a six-figure lifestyle business by the time I was 25. This has created freedom in my life and allows me to spend more time on things that matter like family, friends, and travel, rather than just living to work.

My dad's death, and the changes I made in my life's trajectory and career path as a result, taught me that saving by design (which means having a plan for your money) gives you independence. It is the only way to truly have your actions line up with your words when it comes to loving your family. This book shares my lessons learned and will show you how to begin saving by design to ensure that both you and your family live your absolute best lives.

If you picked this book up because you're looking for another budgeting worksheet or my opinion on what percentage of your income should go towards savings, you're in the wrong place. Saving by design is personal; it's not about following cookie-cutter advice doled out by one of the talking heads on TV or using a worksheet from a personal finance book or magazine. It starts with your personal goals and objectives and means having a strategy to get you what you want in life. That might mean saving 10 percent or it might mean 30 percent. There is no rule of thumb because generic advice doesn't take into consideration your lifestyle or what you actually care about the way a personalized plan does.

I also want to be clear before we dive in that this book is not for those who expect the government, their companies, or their families to take care of them; people who are satisfied with the status quo; or people who love themselves more than their families and aren't afraid to say it. This is also not for people who truly believe that their next stock pick, business success, or winning lottery ticket will be the magic bullet that will change their financial situation forever.

This book is intended for those people out there who want to start saving like they love their family, who want to be confident they're giving their family the best they possibly can with the resources they have. It's for business owners and business leaders who are busy balancing working hard and spending time with those who matter. They know that even though they're making great money because of how hard they work, they should have more to show for it. They know that ignoring their finances has been costing them time, money, and opportunity, and that now is as good a time as any to finally give their financial situation the attention it deserves. They want things to be different. They're tired of their money situation not mirroring their success in other areas of life. If this is you, I'm here to help.

CHAPTER 1

Life Happens

"Life is what happens to you when you're busy making other plans."
—John Lennon

A few years ago, I was car shopping and ended up at the Mercedes dealership. Anyone who knows me knows that somehow, even at Wal-Mart, I manage to gravitate towards the most expensive items. I don't know what it is; I just do! So you can imagine that a visit to the Mercedes dealership was a pretty dangerous proposition. I wasn't there for a Mercedes, though; I was there for an older-model used Cadillac that I saw for a steal online.

Of course once I got there I fell in love with a different car and left with a Benz. Shockingly enough I got a great deal and ended up paying the same price for it as I paid for my old Buick—plus I got a 1.99 percent interest rate, which is so low it might as well have been 0 percent. I was reveling in my good fortune when my salesman told me it was time to meet with the finance manager about warranties. Another thing my friends and family know about me: I'm paranoid and always buy the warranties. This time was different, though. These were warranties for a Mercedes, and to get the ones I knew I should get would have cost me one-third of the price of the car! So I took the GAP insurance and the extended warranty—but not the wheel and tire warranty. Off I went.

I bought my car in December. It was a rough winter, even by Boston standards. In February, the cold was still brutal and it was time for my first car service. Business was great, and I had managed to save some extra money, so I decided to get an automatic starter installed as a late Christmas present to myself at the same time they were doing the oil change. I dropped my car at the dealership, but I'm sure you can guess what happened next. A few hours later, I got a call from my service representative telling me that I had a bubble in my tire and that one of my rims was bent. No sweat, I thought, because I *always* get the wheel and tire warranty. I live right outside of Boston, where there are potholes *everywhere*; why wouldn't I have gotten the wheel and tire warranty? Oh yeah, because it was $1,300! But guess how much the tire and rim replacement would cost? $1,600! The warranty was cheaper than one incident, and I knew if I hit one more pothole I was toast.

So what did I do? When I picked the car up, I ended up paying for my automatic starter, basic service, and a new wheel and a straightened rim (since there was no way in hell I was paying $1,250 for one tire rim). There was also the wheel and tire warranty, which still cost $1,300. I dropped my car off dreaming of a nice warm car in the mornings. Later, I picked it up with the reality of a bill for $2,000 more than I expected to pay and a rim that likely would need to be replaced in the future. In the end I regretted getting the starter; it seemed crazy to spend over $1,000 for the luxury of not having to get into a cold car ever again at the same time I was faced with the necessity of not having my tire blow.

Now, you might be sitting there criticizing every piece of my story. That's what a lot of people do; they comment on the decisions of others *constantly*, especially *after* something happens. (This is especially true on the internet.) I'm sure you wouldn't have bought a Mercedes to begin with because you'd know how much more expensive service and maintenance would be. Or you would have bought it but bit the bullet and chosen the warranty from the get-go. I bet you never would have made any of the same decisions I did. Automatic starter? Stop being a baby and go start your car in the morning like a normal human being!

If you wouldn't have been caught dead spending an extra $2,000 at the dealership two months after you bought your car, I'm willing to bet there's been another situation where you did the exact same thing I did, cheapening out on some aspect of a purchase because of cost, regardless of how it much it might cost you later, or making a decision that ended up continually coming back to haunt you because the right answer was so clear in hindsight.

Think back to a financial mistake you've made that you know cost you money. Did it change the way you've made decisions since then? I'd be willing to bet that your lesson in hindsight has changed how you make decisions around that particular area of your life; you have no choice because you can still remember the pain and you're afraid it will happen again. Maybe you paid $50 to the guy down the street to do your taxes, and then you got audited and owed $6,000 plus a fine, so now you go to a CPA whom you pay $300 instead. You're never going to an amateur for tax prep again, just like I'm never passing up the wheel and tire warranty again.

So you learned your lesson about taxes or another situation, but I'm guessing that experience hasn't changed your decision-making process in other areas. I've learned that the right decision in a given situation is not always apparent, because after we suffer the negative consequences of a decision, fear plays a role in future decision-making. Money is so intertwined with the things we care about, like lifestyle choices and the ability to help both ourselves and others, that we deal with money using emotion instead of logic. This is why getting expert advice when it comes to your money decisions is so crucial.

While it's true that money isn't everything, it does touch everything that's important in our lives. You and I both make decisions around money every single day, and even one bad money decision can have huge implications, so imagine the impact of one or several bad decisions per year. The extra $700 that I spent on the tire and rim because I didn't have the warranty could have grown to $15,000 in my Roth IRA over 40 years.[1]

We've been through two economic bubbles and two crashes in the past two decades. It is natural that many young people have been spooked and scared away from investing in the stock market. This volatility has created more conversation around finances and how vulnerable we are to economic and environmental changes. If you managed to come through

---

1   Had I invested that money in stocks, bonds, or mutual funds averaging 8% annual returns net of fees.

unscathed, you probably know someone who lost their job, business, retirement, or home, and you've seen how some people were able to recover and some were devastated. Observing the crises of those close to us should provide the knowledge and motivation we need to prevent a crisis of our own, but it doesn't. Many of us don't plan even when we see life go wrong for so many others because we think it will never happen to us. But you should know by now that if there's anything you can ever count on, it's that something will go wrong.

Observing the financial devastation of others and being impacted in various ways personally has brought attention to the need for greater financial education and awareness. Many people now understand that financial savvy is one of the top skills necessary to thrive in the 21st century. Financial savvy allows you to make wise financial decisions for your family and your business that can give you the lifestyle you desire. Without it, you're at the mercy of your environment—whether that be people who unintentionally cost you because of their inexperience or lack of knowledge (like the cheap tax preparer), people who intentionally cost you by taking advantage through selling the wrong product or a bad or low-quality product, or missed opportunities that cost you in the long run. This could include not being able to invest in an amazing opportunity or not being able to get a sick family member the best care that would make the difference between months together and years together.

Some of your money decisions will have negative consequences that could have never been predicted. You simply cannot live your life in constant fear, always being overcautious to avoid making bad decisions, because that's no life. But what you can do is minimize the number and severity of your bad money decisions with proper planning. The difference that planning can make is the difference between financial and lifestyle abundance and financial and lifestyle struggle. But at the end of the day, I don't particularly care what happens to you if you don't care what happens to you. If you don't want to live your best life, alleviate stress, and enjoy the benefits of your hard work, then I can't force you to want it or do what it takes to achieve it, no matter how clearly I see the benefit. You should care. Be selfish. It's okay to want the best for yourself and do the work to get it, and there's nothing wrong with being smart and not wasting your resources.

What I do care about is the impact your actions have on those around you. I opened the book by sharing my belief that if you don't plan, you don't love your family, and that if you love your family, you need to save like it. Your kids or future kids are the ones who primarily suffer when you don't take the personal responsibility to teach them right and wrong, both directly and indirectly. And if you don't plan to have kids, you're even worse off, because if you don't plan, your siblings (who likely have their own kids), parents, and close friends are the ones who have to shoulder the burden of your lack of planning. You and I both know that kids learn much more than what you teach them—they see and hear everything. They catch the nuances and they hear the "we can't afford that" or "you overdrafted the accounts again?" conversations.

Many parents aren't teaching their kids simple and common-sense financial principles like "spend less than you make" and "pay yourself first" because they simply don't do it themselves. They also don't realize that just because they're not having smart financial conversations with their kids doesn't mean the kids aren't learning from their actions. What kids learn from their parents' behavior with money carries all the way into adulthood and can mean the difference between success and struggle for them. In fact, if you were to poll your friends, family, and coworkers and ask them the one thing they wish their parents had taught them, I'm willing to bet an overwhelming majority would say they wish their parents had taught them about money.

I don't have kids, not yet at least! But I do know how much my clients and my extended family members love theirs and want the best for them. I do know that just as it's hard to help your kids with homework when they're doing what looks like calculus in the second grade, it's hard to help your kids with money habits when you feel completely out of your element. I also know that it's your responsibility as a parent to educate yourself and your kids the right way.

The reason this hits home so strongly for me, and the reason I'm so passionate about getting you to understand the importance of being financially responsible, isn't only because of my experience with my dad. My dad did pretty well overall. My gripes are mainly about the lack of time spent with us and his heavy emphasis on working yourself to the bone at the expense of those you love. My dad didn't have a financial plan and wasn't working with a financial advisor. In fact, he was one of the cheapest people I know, and would likely never hire one if he were still alive, because he was a smart guy and believed he could figure it out on his own and do just as well, even though all that extra time wasted trying to figure it out wasn't worth it.

But guess what? He was actually one of the few people that worked out for. Why? Because he died at the age of 47 and had a decent life insurance policy, all of his kids were teenagers or older, and my mom was making a very good income and had a specific skill set that allowed her to choose whether to continue working or to take a break and grieve. We didn't care that he didn't have a properly diversified portfolio and that all the random stocks he picked had tanked; because of that insurance policy, we didn't need them. My mom had the luxury of being able to ride out the market, learn about investments, and do her own planning with the help of an excellent financial advisor at the local bank. She ended up selling most of the stocks at a profit and changing her investment strategy when it made the most sense, thus changing our family's story.

Would it have been optimal if all his hard-earned retirement and other savings were invested according to a plan all along so that my mom could have had more leverage that for her retirement later? Yes, it would have been nice. Maybe she could have had extra money to create a scholarship or foundation in his name, but she was fine without it. It worked out for our family, but do you really want to be like my dad and take a gamble, hoping that some random conventional wisdom works out for your family? Or do you want to plan and be able to weather whatever comes?

We all know things happen, but for the most part we're in denial about the importance of planning. Very often the process of planning itself, much like buying insurance or getting your will done, costs money and therefore would require some level of sacrifice. When you won't receive any immediate benefit from spending that money other than peace of mind, it's easy to either procrastinate on the planning or never do it at all.

There are very real and immediate costs associated with not planning that many people don't even realize because of a lack of financial education. For one, people send too much money to the government in the form of taxes—not just the money they are paying today, but the money they set themselves up to owe in the future. There are strategies to keep more of that money in your pocket, but it requires planning.

Many people are also sending way too much money to insurance companies, banks, and investment companies for things like interest, fees and charges, insurance premiums for the wrong kinds of insurance, or insurance policies and product fees that are altogether unnecessary. It has nothing to do with those companies being bad or evil; it has to do with the fact that those companies are set up to make themselves money and people don't set up their financial lives to maximize their return on investment. Many people don't think they spend a lot of money on these things; they either don't notice or just think the costs are unavoidable. Maybe you've had the same car insurance policy for years and never thought to look into a better rate but there is an option to save $500 per year. Maybe you're putting an extra $150 towards your mortgage to round things out, but you're carrying credit card debt that is costing you 4 times the mortgage interest. In reality, the costs associated with any of these extend far beyond the extra fees, taxes, charges, and unnecessary insurance premiums paid. The greater cost is in the lost opportunities that money could have a provided. The average American family losing $200 per month as a result of one or a combination of the factors above translates to over $5 million[2] over the course of their lifetime. That's a lot of money! What if you're unwittingly losing more than that? Wouldn't you rather keep that money for yourself and your family?

A few years after Daddy died, the true magnitude of the importance of planning really became clear to me. It shifted the way I look at planning. It was first thing in the morning and I was driving to meet a client at my office when I got a call from a number I didn't recognize. It was a hospital in Rhode Island saying my sister had gotten into an accident the night before, had broken her neck, and was in the hospital with pretty severe injuries. My heart stopped and I was overcome with dread and panic. All I could think of was that my family couldn't handle another tragedy so soon after losing my dad. They then put my sister, who was crying hysterically, on the phone so she could tell me a bit of what had happened and ask me to come get her. I cancelled my appointments for the day, immediately grateful that being self-employed meant I could be there for my family without worrying about losing my job or being penalized for it.

---

2   An average of $200 per month from age 24 to age 90 invested at 8% on average translates to , $5,173,704.

My sister was in school when her accident happened. Lots of adjustments had to be made in the aftermath. In addition to dealing with severe pain, she was in a wheelchair and a neck brace for months after the accident. Her mobility was compromised and it took her longer than expected to finish her undergraduate degree. Her student healthcare—which she'd gotten through school like many students do—wasn't great, and my mom had moved back home to Montreal where we grew up, so there was no backup insurance. The bills associated with surgery, rehab, and other accident-related costs were extremely high; there was no way that my sister as a college junior could have paid for them. Had my mom not been able to pay the cost of the bills either, my sister would have been saddled with a huge debt that could have impacted her ability to start her life after college - and she might have had to make decisions about her care based on affordability instead of who could best put the pieces back together.

Unfortunately, even after my sister "healed" (meaning she could go back to living life basically as she was before), nothing was the same as it had been before the accident and there was still severe financial impact. An injury as severe as breaking your neck affects your whole body, and even after it heals you're never quite the same. The accident was over three years ago and my sister still goes to chiropractic and acupuncture multiple times per week. She gets massages and sees other specialists as well because she's always in pain and it impacts her ability to do everything she wants and needs to do. What's worse, she has chosen to do work she loves but that doesn't pay well and doesn't have great benefits. The providers that she's seen the most improvement with aren't in-network on her insurance, and because she desperately wants to get better she has been relentless about finding the best care regardless of whether her insurance will cover it, so she spends every penny of her income on services to help her get better. When she's not working, she's seeing healthcare providers both traditional and alternative, or she's going back and forth with her insurance companies to get coverage for her care.

Who would have thought that an accident would have so impacted my sister that she would still be paying for it financially, physically, and emotionally four years later? The only way she can get the full care she needs based on her circumstances is for me and my mom to help out. My sister lives with me and doesn't have to pay rent, utilities, or her cell phone bill, and my mom and I help cover certain services, but the only reason we can do that is because we're not among the 69 percent of Americans who have less than $1,000 in savings.[3] That's right—nearly seven out of every ten people in the United States has managed to save less than $250 per family member in their household. Think about that. You might be thinking, "Who cares if they don't have that money in savings! That doesn't mean Americans aren't saving, the money is probably in investment accounts." I wanted to believe that too, but unfortunately the statistics on retirement savings are just as bleak. According to the Economic Policy Institute (EPI), nearly half of families have no retirement savings at all and many of those who do don't have very much.[4] If you're in this boat don't beat yourself up too much—you're clearly not alone—but think about this for a minute.

How much money do you have in savings? I am referring to true savings—savings for an emergency, not money in your checking account, or money in a savings account but earmarked for something you already know you need to pay for, or money in a retirement account or set aside for another specific goal. Are you financially responsible for at least one other person? This could be a child, sibling, parent, or spouse/significant other—this could be anyone who relies on you for some kind of financial support or commitment, no matter how small you think that support is. What would be the implications if you suffered financially and could no longer help that person? Or worse, what would happen if your financial circumstances were what they are today and that person got in an accident or got sick and required care?

Be honest with your answers to those questions. These things happen every single day. Maybe if something happened right now you truly wouldn't be able to help, or you would be able to only if you cut back, making significant changes to your lifestyle. If you're not satisfied with your answers to those questions, don't let your embarrassment or shame prevent you from taking action and doing something different. This may all seem vague and hypothetical, but a study done by Harvard and published in the American Journal of Health revealed medical bills

---

3   USA Today, "Nearly 7 in 10 Americans have less than $1,000 in Savings" October 29, 2016

4   Economic Policy Institute, "The State of American Retirement" March 3, 2016 www.epi.org/publication/retirement-in-america. Nearly half of families have no retirement account savings at all. That makes median (50th percentile) values low for all age groups, ranging from $480 for families in their mid-30s to $17,000 for families approaching retirement in 2013.

are not as the number 1 cause of bankruptcy at 61 percent of filings, with 72 percent of those individuals having had medical insurance at the time of filing.[5] If you're curious, other top causes of bankruptcy include job loss, excessive use of credit/spending habits, and divorce. Do you still feel bulletproof?

Planning is so foreign to many people because until recently failure to plan didn't have such high consequences, so there wasn't such a big emphasis on personal responsibility. Many people learned that the most important thing was to get a good job with a good company that offered great benefits. If you did that and worked for them for most, if not all, of your career, you would receive a pension that, coupled with Social Security, would cover your retirement needs. Many people today don't realize that 401(k) plans only came out in the 1980s; companies offered them to employees as a way to put away a little extra pre-tax money that they could use for their retirement lifestyles. Many people took advantage of this because they saw the benefit of being able to sock away some extra money that would grow and then be withdrawn when they were in a lower tax bracket in retirement.

At that time, the conventional wisdom was also to buy a house instead of renting, because a house was an investment. People would buy a home and pay the mortgage. By the time they retired the mortgage would be paid off and the house they raised their kids in would be worth significantly more than they had bought it for. Because many people didn't jump around much from job to job, work benefits including health insurance, life insurance, and disability insurance were pretty sufficient and supplemental coverage wasn't as important. People also didn't live as long back then so retirement was simple; it lasted 10–15 years and then they'd pass away of old age and not necessarily because of a long, drawn-out sickness. Because in many ways life was simpler back then and there were more guarantees, so to speak, it was easier for people to save a bit of money for a rainy day and spend the rest on the things they enjoyed.

---

5   Clinical Research Study, The American Journal of Health, "Medical Bankruptcy in the United States, 2007: Results of a National Study" David U. Himmelstein, MD, Deborah Thorne, PhD, Elizabeth Warren, JD, Steffie Woolhandler, MD, MPH

Fast-forward to the present day. We see today that things are a mess for those approaching retirement now and those who will come after. A lot has shifted very quickly and we seem to have just accepted it as how things are without really questioning the vast implications of these changes on our financial lives until it's too late. Those who are nearing retirement and didn't adjust to the changing times are often forced to work well past the traditionally accepted retirement age of 65, and those who will reach retirement age in the coming decades are, for the most part, ill-equipped financially.

As a matter of fact, only 4 percent of Americans say they think they are ready for retirement. Close to half of Americans aged 55–64 have no retirement plan at all,[6] and will need a part-time job to meet their basic expenses. Guess what? That's not retirement; as least not as it was traditionally defined for generations. Rather than anticipating a retirement filled with golf, travel, time spent with grandchildren, and friends, the lack of preparation for retirement leads to anxiety about the necessity of building a business or being able to consult and continue working out of necessity, but looking to do so in a less demanding and stressful environment than they spent their pre-retirement years in. There is a big difference between having the luxury of working or volunteering if you choose in your retirement years and between needing to work to maintain the same standard of living as before retirement which is often more chaotic than leisurely. Many Americans are increasingly turning to some form of work, even if part-time or sporadic in nature, to help subsidize their Golden Years. Many find that they prefer to find ways to remain productive, with science pointing to health and wellness benefits for those who remain engaged in meaningful work. However, it is hard to predict what your mindset will be regarding whether or not you still want to be working in your advanced years. Saving and planning now will provide you more flexibility and freedom to make such choices on your own terms – rather than being forced to return to work to make ends meet.

---

6   Report to the Ranking Member, Subcommittee on Primary Health and Retirement Security, Committee on Health, Education, Labor, and Pensions, U.S. Senate by the U.S. Government Accountability Office, "RETIREMENT SECURITY: Most Households Approaching Retirement Have Low Savings" May 2015

The reality is that the support system that we have designed for retirement is from an era that no longer exists. The majority of companies don't offer pensions these days, and of those that do, many of them offer pensions that are employee funded from paycheck contributions instead of being solely an employer-provided benefit. Towers Watson, a leading global professional services company, has done in depth analysis and tracking over the past 15 years of trends in the retirement offerings of the top US companies—those that make up the Fortune 500.[7] The result of their analysis is the shocking statistic that between 1998 and 2013, the percentage of those top employers offering traditional pensions where the responsibility is on the employer, to fulfill a defined benefit to their employees in retirement dropped from roughly 50 percent to 7 percent. These are the country's top companies based on revenue, i.e. they are the companies with the most money, and they won't even offer these benefits anymore. Some of you are thinking you're in the public sector, so you're safe. Don't be too sure. Another issue with the pensions that are still around is that it's harder to rely on them. Nothing is guaranteed anymore. Many pension funds have been mismanaged, and the employees who expected their company pensions to supplement Social Security are now left to worry about the viability of the companies they chose to spend their lives working for and their employer's ability to pay the promised benefits. Just last year, the city of Chicago was in and out of court contending that it was not legally on the hook to pay pensions. Just because you work for a city or state and a pension is offered, doesn't mean the funds will be there when you're ready to retire.

The swift disappearance of pensions for over 75 percent of Americans has meant that a key source of retirement income is now gone. The 401(k) is a widely used and familiar tool, but following the conventional wisdom of using a 401(k) to defer taxes owed now and paying them in retirement is likely not the most beneficial solution for many of us. Because federal taxes are the lowest that they have been in decades, tax rates are likely to continue creeping up—which means you'll likely pay more tax (on more money) when you take it out than you would right now. In addition, many people aren't saving enough in any retirement vehicle to be able to replace their income to the extent that pensions used to, so their retirements are vastly underfunded.

---

7   Willis Towers Watson, "Defined Contribution Plan Volatility: Timing Is Everything," Towers Watson Insider, September 2015.

When you look at home ownership, we no longer see most mortgages being paid off by retirement. In fact, the average American isn't buying a home, staying in it for the rest of his or her life, and keeping it in the family. Instead, the average American today moves 11.4 times.[8] Do you know how expensive moving is? And when we talk about a home as an investment, we fail to talk about the impact of the housing crash that we have yet to recover from. There has never been another time in history when people were so underwater on their mortgages, trapped in homes that no longer fit their lifestyles, or that they can't afford – not assets, but liabilities.

The trend of working for the same employer for your entire career has also shifted, with the average American changing jobs every 4.4 years according to the Bureau of Labor Statistics. That translates to about seven job changes for the average American. Often people change jobs for better opportunities, and sometimes it's because life circumstances have changed or the employer lets them go for whatever reason. Regardless of why these moves are happening, the shift from working for the same company forever to jumping around means that an individual's work benefits are constantly changing. There is no standard benefits package for every company, so job-hopping often leads to lost benefits that aren't immediately or ever replaced by the new employer. This has created a significant need for private benefits that no one talks much about.

Aside from health insurance, two of the key insurance benefits offered at many large employers are life insurance and disability insurance. Both are vital to the financial success of many families should something happen, but qualifying for such benefits is heavily dependent on an individual's health, and we often don't think about it until it's too late. As young people entering the workforce, we're less likely to enroll in those standard benefits because we feel invincible, like nothing will ever happen to us. Trust me, I can relate to that feeling. I've always considered myself pretty healthy. I'm athletic, I eat well, and I pay attention to my body- slowing down or sleeping more when I need to recharge. Like everyone else, I never thought anything would happen to me. But it did.

---

8   US Census Bureau, "FOR IMMEDIATE RELEASE: WEDNESDAY, MARCH 18, 2015." U.S. Mover Rate Remains Stable at About 12 Percent Since 2008", Census Bureau Reports, March 18, 2015, Release Number: CB15-47

In December of last year I was driving home from an early dinner and another driver ran a stop sign and hit my car head on. Not only was my car totaled, but I got a severe concussion and was having memory issues and getting lost for weeks after, Being someone who uses my brain for work, this was terrifying. At the time, I had just decided to move my practice from one company to another and I didn't have a private disability policy because I made the same excuse that I hear people make every day: "I don't do manual labor, and I would need to be pretty severely disabled to not be able to do my job." Well, a concussion makes it pretty hard to work with clients and get around and I was lucky that I practiced what I preach in other areas and had an emergency fund, but it was still a painful process. Yes, I had money, but after paying the expenses associated with moving my practice, a month and a half of being out of work, and now needing to buy another car, my emergency fund was quickly depleted.

You know that saying, "When it rains, it pours"? Well, shortly after this disaster, just as I was getting my footing back, I had a cancer scare… and all of the associated medical bills. Now I was in a position where I needed to work, but I needed to take care of myself too and some big decisions had to be made financially to make everything work that included cashing out some investments. Everything worked out, but it was very clear to me that had I had my own disability insurance policy, timing of jobs would have never been an issue and my emergency fund would have gone down, but my investments never would have needed to be touched. Now, I'm in a position where because of those recent medical issues, I can't apply for my own policy until a sufficient amount of time has passed and that is an incredibly frustrating thing.

Typically, when we're younger, because we think we're invincible we don't plan head and planning only comes in as life changes. As we get older and get married or remarried, or are in a long-term relationship and maybe have kids, at some point we decide enrolling in basic benefits is a smart idea. I've also seen time and time again that when clients work for a company and the company offers benefits, they assume that enrolling in the maximum benefits are enough and is the best idea without understanding the coverage and terms of the benefits. If insurance is offered, and they enroll in the maximum the company offers they think they'll be okay. But they aren't sure, and usually even the max benefits offered at many companies are minimal for those who aren't in the lowest income tiers so for many people there is a resulting gap in both understanding and coverage.

Another danger, like in my personal story, is that we've probably changed jobs along the way. Perhaps our employer doesn't offer a level of coverage sufficient to protect our family's lifestyle, so we look to private options. However, we are older or possibly not as healthy as we were before, making private benefits likely significantly more expensive and maybe even unavailable.

Retirement planning, college planning, deciding whether to buy or rent (and what to buy or rent), and securing private benefits to protect ourselves and our families—let alone saving for a rainy day—feels almost impossible because these changes coincided with a larger shift: from living simple to living large. We don't want to buy the smallest house; have one family car, a basic phone, and basic cable; and take basic vacations. This shift isn't recent; it has happened across all generations since the baby boomers and including some of the boomers. We want houses that we can be proud to raise our families in, two cars that allow us to live our own lives and be individuals, smartphones so we're always connected, premium cable so we can relax at home, and vacations that allow us to experience the world. We want to have the American Dream—and give the same to our kids.

The problem is that for the most part, as a society we are still operating financially according to past assumptions and implementing conventional wisdom in a piecemeal fashion, praying that everything works out. We're paying for things that don't make us money or improve our financial situations, but cheap out on expert advice in areas that truly make a difference. We're also not valuing our time. We're selling our houses on our own on our third move because we don't want to shell out money for a commission, yet hiring a qualified realtor who sells houses every day would get us top dollar and save us spending endless hours—hours that are finite and valuable and could be spent with those who matter—figuring out what the expert already knows.

If I told you that you can have everything you ever wanted and still save for all of your financial goals, no matter what, as long as you have a plan and tailored, experienced and knowledgeable advice, I'd be lying to you. But what a plan and this kind of advice will allow you to do is identify what is most important to you, both now and in the future, and tailor a plan to make sure those top priorities happen, while helping to curb financial mistakes that would otherwise continually set you back. Everything has changed, so it's time to act differently.

Chapter Questions:

Think back to an experience you had similar to my Mercedes experience and write it down. How much did that mistake cost you? Did it change the way you've made decisions since then?

_____

_____

_____

_____

How much money do you have in savings? I am referring to true savings—savings for an emergency, not money in your checking account, or money in a savings account but earmarked for something you already know you need to pay for, or money in a retirement account or set aside for another specific goal.

_____

_____

_____

_____

Are you financially responsible for at least one other person? This could be a child, sibling, parent, or spouse/significant other—make a note of anyone who relies on you for some kind of financial support or commitment, no matter how small you think that support is.

_____

_____

_____

_____

What would be the implications if you suffered financially and could no longer help that person? Or worse, what would happen if your financial circumstances were what they are today and that person got in an accident or got sick and required care?

_____

_____

_____

_____

CHAPTER 2

Act Differently

"Wherever I see people doing something the way it's always been done, the way it's 'supposed' to be done, following the same old trends, well, that's just a big red flag to me to go look somewhere else."
—Mark Cuban

During my last year of college, I was offered a great opportunity to work for a well-known corporate bank in Boston. I was working on a degree in business and was seriously interested in economics and corporate finance, so this was an amazing opportunity—especially since up until then I'd been working in unrelated industries, like retail, that hadn't given me the relevant experience I was looking for. In the first six months at the bank, I learned so much about the industry and so much about myself. I was doing everything I was "supposed" to be doing as a soon-to-be college grad, and many would have killed for the opportunity I had, but I knew I was in the wrong environment.

I realized that I thought differently and that realization struck me to my core.

I wasn't the only one in that program. There were about 25 others who had been selected that year and undergone training with me. We were all in different departments, but there were pockets of us in the same building, so we'd meet for coffee or stop by each other's desks every so often to catch up. Many of us had similar experiences: we were in poorly organized groups with higher-ups that didn't necessarily have the time or bandwidth to train us, so they gave us basic tasks that didn't require much thought or effort and could be completed in far less time than was allotted to us. When some of us would finish tasks quickly and were eager to take on something else, we'd be told to use the entire time frame given to finish the task because the manager didn't have other work to give us. Almost all of us experienced a lot of money talk—people at all different levels complaining about how underpaid they were compared to others at different companies, about bonus freezes, about their inability to go anywhere else because this was 2010 and we'd just had the crash. Even aside from the money talk, there was a palpable feeling of general dissatisfaction.

I knew right off the bat that although I was grateful for the opportunity, something was off. If this was what it meant to find a job at a good company—do your penance, climb the corporate ladder, and eventually be promoted or able to use the expertise to go somewhere else—then I was choosing a different track. I didn't want to do work that was far below my capabilities; I wanted to learn and be challenged. I also didn't want to be in a negative environment. The fact that the salary was low wasn't as much of an issue to me—in fact, I actually thought it was high for what our responsibilities were. I saw very clearly that we were being paid $15 per hour to do work that was worth $10 per hour or less, and because of it I knew instinctively that there would be little leverage for raise negotiations in the future—surely there were others looking for entry-level work in the field who would happily take the $15/hour.

I knew I had to leave, and I knew the only way to get everything I wanted and thought was important at my age, with my experience, and in the current economic environment, was to be my own boss, but that was scary and I didn't know exactly what that business would look like, so I kept the job hunt going. When I'd check in with my peers about what they were going to do when the job offers came, every single one of them—except my closest friend in the program who had a side business and planned to launch that into a full-time endeavor—said they wouldn't take the job—but of course all of them except my friend did take it. But when I got my official job offer, I knew I couldn't accept and declined it before even hearing the proposed salary. Even though I had nothing else lined up, I knew I wouldn't be happy there. I was confident that my work ethic and work experience, even though much of it was unrelated to my desired field, would get me where I needed to go.

> Is there a time where you made a financial decision based on the advice of others and it backfired? Or a time you regret not having taken advantage of what you saw as a financial opportunity because of outside advice? Did the person giving you advice have a stake in your success?

Around the same time, I'd been presented with the idea of building a financial planning practice. There was no salary, only commissions. This meant that my paycheck would be directly determined by how many insurance and investment products I sold and by how big those sales were. I didn't go to college, study pre-med, and graduate at the top of my class with a finance degree to be in sales. I knew that for me, however, self-employment meant freedom. Despite the fact I would be responsible for my own overhead and expenses, I felt that I could at least make what I would have made going full time after my internship. I knew if I couldn't do it and failed, I could always pick myself up, dust myself off, and go back to the drawing board.

I had long talks with several people whom I loved, respected, and trusted about my desire to give it a try. My mom, my close friend Will, my girlfriends, my fiancé—all the people who knew me best. The thing about those who know you best and love you is that they often want to protect you. They don't want you to make a mistake that could hurt you in the long run, and sometimes they don't know how committed or uncommitted you are to the results. My fiancé was the only one out of all the people I consulted who said with full conviction, "If you can't do it, nobody can. If you think you can make the same money or more working for yourself, you'll do it." And I did.

Apple's "Think Different" campaign of the late 1990s and early 2000s resonated with me pretty deeply because I've always felt different. I always think differently than others, and sometimes it's a good thing and sometimes it's a bad thing, but I always find myself challenging the norms. What I've found is that there's a huge difference between thinking differently and acting differently, and that's where the differentiator is. It's not enough to think differently. In a PBS interview several years before the "Think Different" campaign was launched, Steve Jobs said:

When you grow up you tend to get told the world is the way it is and your life is just to live your life inside the world. Try not to bash into the walls too much. Try to have a nice family life, have fun, save a little money.

That's a very limited life. Life can be much broader once you discover one simple fact, and that is—everything around you that you call life was made up by people that were no smarter than you. And you can change it, you can influence it, you can build your own things that other people can use.

The minute that you understand that you can poke life and actually something will, you know if you push in, something will pop out the other side, that you can change it, you can mold it. That's maybe the most important thing. It's to shake off this erroneous notion that life is there and you're just going to live in it, versus embrace it, change it, improve it, make your mark upon it. I think that's very important and however you learn that, once you learn it, you'll want to change life and make it better, because it's kind of messed up, in a lot of ways. Once you learn that, you'll never be the same again.

Can you think of a time where you've thought differently but not acted on it? What were the consequences? What about a time where you did act? The sentiments shared in this excerpt are clearly a call to action, not simply to thought. Thinking alone doesn't build, mold, and change things. But the value of thinking—and acting—differently is clear because there is no one-size-fits-all approach when it comes to anything, money included.

I'm sure you've seen those articles in certain lifestyle magazines that outline the "best haircut" or "best style tips" or "best workouts" for you based on your age bracket. If you see something that says "If you're in your 20s, you'd look great in jeans, but if you're in your 50s, a tunic is the way to go," you probably take it with a grain of salt knowing that just because you're 54 doesn't mean a tunic is the right choice for your body shape. Specific information can never be universal. And although general information can be universal—"to save money, spend less than you make" and "to lose weight, eat less and exercise more"—it often falls short.

> Where do you find yourself comparing yourself to others financially? Is there a friend or neighbor you feel like you can never keep up with? Is that comparison or trying to keep up with them hurting you financially?

With money magazines and general financial advice, you often hear a refrain on the same adages. "If you're in your 20s, make sure you're contributing to your 401(k) up to the match; if you're in your 50s, make sure you're on track to pay off your house by your desired retirement date." Those aren't necessarily bad pieces of advice; if your statistics are exactly like those of the sample in your age bracket. In fact, if you fit the profile of the group being addressed to a T and you decide to follow that advice because you've educated yourself on all the options and are confident that that's the best option for you, it's likely that you'll be fine and things will work out pretty well. The trouble is that many people don't take an accurate self-assessment to find out where they are compared to their peers, and they don't educate themselves enough about the topic to be able to determine the best option.

Another saying that we have all heard so often that we don't even internalize it anymore is, "Just because everyone else is doing it doesn't mean you should." It's basic, but very true on many levels. And even though we all know we shouldn't, we often gauge our progress or success based on how well those around us are doing. We're in a constant state of comparison. Some think they're doing much worse than others their age and some think they're doing much better, but much of what they're basing that on is perception and not facts. Unfortunately, it's easy to see whether you're over- or underweight compared to your peers just by looking around at your ten-year class reunion. It is much harder to gauge where you fall financially purely through observation because there is a stigma around money and things aren't always as they appear.

I have a client who I have been working with for several years who falls into a profile in which following the conventional wisdom has served her particularly well. Let's call her Betty.

Betty worked at the same company for over 40 years, has a substantial pension that replaces over 60 percent of her income, and qualifies for Social Security. She's done well within the old financial environment I talked about earlier. Betty has also always been a good saver, so when the 401(k) came out and her company offered that along with a deferred compensation option, she enrolled in both and began contributing money every paycheck. All her life, whenever she heard about opportunities that made sense for her, she took advantage.

She also had good financial habits and has always paid herself first—putting some money into her personal savings and then spending the rest—so that if she wanted to help her kids out, or go on a family vacation, or retire a few years early, she was also able to without any issues. Don't get me wrong; not every decision she's made financially has been the right one. She followed general advice that worked out, but she didn't receive specific advice which could have helped get her further, and may have been more efficient from a cost and effort perspective.

Betty saved for retirement but didn't have a properly diversified portfolio. She regrets only taking advantage of contributing to a Roth IRA during the last year she worked before retirement. Based on what she wants to happen in different scenarios, she also didn't purchase the right amounts on her insurance policies when she was young and healthy, so looking at supplements when we were retirement planning was painful for her. That being said, none of her financial slipups have impacted her ability to have the lifestyle she wants in retirement. With her pension and Social Security she is able to continue to save and hasn't needed to touch her retirement savings in the almost three years she's been retired.

Not every 66-year-old has this experience and is as fortunate and disciplined. Had this woman not had her pension to rely on, I'm not sure she would have saved enough over her working years to be in the same position now, and we'll never know. But the point is, not everyone needs a financial advisor to end up okay. Some people can and will go through life with no professional advice and no understanding of personal finance and they will make it to retirement and be able to say they lived a great life, went on vacation, and were able to help their kids; implementing a few pieces of financial advice here and there about saving and spending will be sufficient to get them there. Unfortunately, however, many people won't fare so well; they will end up living a less-than-ideal lifestyle at times and will have to make decisions out of necessity based on their financial position rather than based on what they want for themselves and their families.

I'm a millennial who doesn't fit the profile of many of my peers, so not only do I see where generic advice and conventional wisdom have failed my clients, but I see it very clearly for myself when I read money advice targeted at my generation. Much of the conversation around millennials doesn't apply to me. I'm an entrepreneur who has been earning six figures running my practice since I graduated from college. I'm not worried about finding a job or losing my job because I created my own. I also don't live with my parents; I live in one unit of a multi-family home that brings in rental income, and I'm able to provide a place to stay for my three siblings when they need it. Because I'm financially stable, I'm able to invest in continuing education related to my practice as well as strategy around successful entrepreneurship in general. I'm also able to help my siblings financially if necessary and, thanks to the flexibility I have as an entrepreneur, I am able to be there for them emotionally and physically when life happens and something goes wrong.

I'm also a spender, and I don't feel bad about it—even though others who don't save and invest the way I do often comment on my lifestyle. I travel, a lot. I'd rather spend my money on a month in Southeast Asia with my two best girlfriends from college rather than on Starbucks, nightclubs, and expensive nights drinking at bars. Everyone's preferences are different. I know what my priorities are and I'd rather experience life now than try to retire by 40. I don't personally care about early retirement; I love being an entrepreneur. Those are my life choices.

Because I know I don't fit into the milieu of the typical millennial, I don't follow most general advice, and instead I work hard to seek out the answers that work for me and leverage the advice of professionals. In fact, my life would be much different had I listened to what other people were saying and the general advice being given to me four years ago, instead of taking the road less traveled and trusting my gut, hiring professional advice, and doing some digging. I can say pretty confidently that had I not taken the risk to start my practice, I'd be in a master's program right now studying to be a doctor, working a few hourly jobs part-time to get a full-time paycheck to pay the bills, and racking up student loans. I wouldn't be traveling and I wouldn't be able to help my siblings, because I frankly wouldn't be in the position to. Would I have a bad life? Of course not. But it just goes to show the power of the decisions we make every day.

The rest of this book will address the problems outlined so far, which boil down to the damage of failing to plan and implementing piecemeal conventional wisdom that doesn't hold up anymore and general financial advice that isn't tailored to your situation. I'll walk you through common advice related to personal finance that many people never question and break it down so you can see where this advice works in your life and where it doesn't work so that you're better able to customize a strategy for yourself and your family.

Because I want you to feel free to skip around, here is a breakdown of what each chapter will cover:

Chapter 3: Ignore the Noise

- Cost versus price: more expensive doesn't mean it costs more

- The right information is better than more information

- Never take unsolicited advice about your lifestyle choices

- Don't take general advice about investments and financial strategy

Chapter 4: Wealth versus Money

- Wealth is not about being a millionaire or having tons of money

- Wealth is subjective, not one size fits all

- You can't build true wealth without personal goals and objectives

Chapter 5: Save Smarter, Not Harder

- How to create leverage in your financial life

- Why percentages won't get you financial freedom

- How to get clear on where you're saving hard, not smart

Chapter 6: The Real Estate Myth

- Why your home may not be a good investment

- How to figure out whether your house is an asset or a liability

- Real estate investing and how to use it to create leverage

Chapter 7: The Entrepreneurship Trap

- Self-employment myths

- Why many entrepreneurs have the worst financial situations

- Multi-level business models and why many people say they're a rip-off

Chapter 8: Stop Living in Denial

- What now?

- Are you willing to change?

Chapter Questions:

Is there a time where you made a financial decision based on the advice of others and it backfired? Or a time you regret not having taken advantage of what you saw as a financial opportunity because of outside advice? Did the person giving you advice have a stake in your success?

_____

_____

_____

_____

Can you think of a time where you've thought differently but not acted on it? What were the consequences? What about a time where you did act?

_____

_____

_____

_____

Where do you find yourself comparing yourself to others financially? Is there a friend or neighbor you feel like you can never keep up with? Is that comparison or trying to keep up with them hurting you financially?

_____

_____

_____

_____

CHAPTER 3

Ignore the Noise

"If you think it's expensive to hire a professional, just wait until you hire an amateur."
—Mark Cuban

You're driving down the street in your car, hit a pothole, and your tire goes flat. It just so happens that upon inspection of the damage, you realize that your rim is also bent. You remember from my story that a new rim and tire on that car will run you about $1,600 and that straightening the rim will cost $700. There is no way you can afford that right now so you call your brother, who knows more about cars than you do, to ask his advice. He tells you to get a tire from a discount tire shop in town and have your car towed to a local mechanic he's heard is pretty affordable who can straighten the rim, and that if it turns out the rim can't be straightened, you should order a rim online. You call AAA for a tow to the mechanic's shop.

The mechanic is able to straighten your rim and replace your tire the next afternoon, and you end up paying $500 total, which is $200 less than what the dealership would have charged you. You drive away from the mechanic's so happy that you were able to get a great deal. A few weeks later, your new tire pops. Turns out that rim was too damaged to be straightened and now you need a new tire *and* a new rim, and if you order them yourself you'll also need to pay for a rental because the dealership only covers rentals when they're doing the service. Even worse?

The mechanic refuses to take any responsibility for the issue and is going to charge you for the labor on the new tire and rim change and alignment.

Have you ever had an incident like that? I've had so many it's hard to keep track, because when I was younger the biggest factor for me was how much things cost. I've been working since high school - for me, money has always come with obligations. Money allowed me to be more independent—to get a car, rent an apartment, buy a house—and all of those things cost more money. It got to the point where I felt so out of control because it seemed like one thing after another would pop up that cost money and I was never prepared. I grew up in a family that placed more emphasis on cost than value, so it was easy to feel like I was being financially savvy by shopping around for services and hiring someone who charged less. I found time and time again that I was wrong, but that I wasn't alone.

Stop hiring amateurs. What exactly is an amateur? In some cases, it's someone who performs the work but isn't considered an expert of the profession, like the difference between an amateur athlete and a professional. In other cases, an amateur is someone who is completely inept at that profession or activity. In many cases, the amateurs I'm referring to are the former. You hire a mechanic that isn't the best but is the cheapest. If it's just an oil change, you might be okay. But if you take your car to him for something more complicated, you might end up paying double because you have to go to the more expensive expert mechanic to fix the damage the amateur mechanic caused and finally solve your problem.

We've all been burned by a person or product because our priority was cost, not value, and we were willing to take a risk. Sometimes we do it not only because of price but because the amateur is a friend, we want to support them, and we're hoping they take extra pains to do the job right because of that relationship. Sometimes it works out, sometimes it doesn't.

Another type of amateur is someone who doesn't have a real stake in your personal, professional, or financial success. We've all been subject to this: the opinions of well-meaning friends, family, colleagues, and even strangers who want to help us. Unfortunately, that friend that tells you to quit your job because of an issue you're having with your boss isn't going to put food on the table if you listen to her and don't have a way to replace the lost income. The guy at work who tells you to move all of your investments into cash (even though he doesn't have investments of his own) doesn't suffer when the market rebounds but your retirement portfolio doesn't.

> When was the last time you got burned by acting on advice given by someone who wasn't an expert in the field or by hiring a lower-cost service provider? What did you learn from the experience?

The fact of the matter is that many professionals have a reputation to uphold. They are getting paid for their services and they are running businesses based on expertise. Oftentimes, they actually do have a stake in your success, because if you experience success as a result of working with them you will likely hire them again and recommend that others do the same. If you have a poor experience with them, they not only lose future business but they also typically pay a cost associated with trying to make things right. In terms of financial advisors in particular, some are also held to fiduciary standards, which means they are charged with putting their clients' best interests ahead of their own.

Price has become a huge factor for people these days, so much so that the conversation often happens independently of a discussion on value. This is a *huge* issue because the price of something rarely indicates the true cost. We make money decisions every day. Money literally touches every aspect of our lives, so our behaviors and daily money decisions have the power to make or break our financial position and lifestyle goals. How you make your money decisions is crucial, and a consistent focus on price and not cost can be devastating.

Much of what I've accomplished up to this point in my life, both personally and professionally, can be attributed to the fact that I ignored the noise. I chose to consider the opinions of others I trusted and respected without blindly accepting them, and after weighing all of the options and opinions I chose to take the road less traveled, which was what my intuition and knowledge told me was right for me. I was lucky to have one person at that time that supported my decision, which unfortunately isn't the case for everyone.

I received advice from friends and family who knew the risks associated with my decision to pursue entrepreneurship, as well as advice from "experts" I came across while doing my due diligence. These weren't amateurs, they actually were experts, but they weren't experts on my situation; I hadn't hired them to figure out the viability of what I was trying to do based on my strengths and weaknesses. They were giving advice to the general public, and what they said was probably true for more than half of their target audience, but if what they said was wrong for me and I followed the advice anyway, they weren't taking responsibility for the associated costs.

> When was the last time you looked at the true cost of a bad decision instead of just looking at the price paid? What were the hidden costs?

These well-regarded, well-respected experts cautioned against entrepreneurship without certain safety nets in place. Their general advice gave a million reasons I shouldn't do it: I didn't have adequate savings, the success rate for financial advisors is very low, I was young with no network and no experience as a small business owner, and I had a job with a guaranteed paycheck. All of the advice was logical, but it was also money focused and was looking at the price, which was a lost $35,000 salary plus benefits, and not the overall cost.

In fact, the cost of me staying at that job and potentially going back to school part-time initially while I got on my feet—instead of starting my practice—would have been over $100,000 per year every year that I was in business. There is also a huge value to be assigned to freedom, independence, and the growth I've experienced as a person in becoming a business owner.

Although people you know directly or indirectly, and whom you trust, may be intelligent or successful in areas of their lives—maybe even the same areas you aspire to success in—you shouldn't make your financial or personal decisions based on others' advice unless they are truly experts in their field and you are willing to pay for the value they bring to your decisions. That's because the only people who suffer the consequences or pay the cost of those decisions are you and the people who love you and depend on you.

Many people operate financially based on the advice of amateurs and the generic advice of experts who don't know their actual financial situation and personal goals. The reason we typically operate this way is because we were taught about cost at a young age, both directly ("You can't have that game; it's too expensive") and indirectly (through choices made about where to live, what to drive, and whom to hang out with), but weren't necessarily taught about good money behaviors and the concepts of quality and value. Many of us didn't learn financial savvy growing up because our parents didn't have it and couldn't teach it, so it's natural to be intimidated by our finances and feel like victims of our financial situations.

> Who was the last person you took financial advice from that wasn't a professional? Why did you trust that person to give you that advice? Looking back, are you still confident that they were qualified to give the advice? Why? Is that only based on the advice having worked out for you, or do they actually have background that qualifies them?

You feel like you're doing all the right things, but for some reason you always feel behind the eight ball. And then you look around at your peers and for the most part they're going on vacations, achieving success at work, and seem to know something you don't. It's natural to assume that they must be doing something differently, and if you knew what it was you could use that to improve your situation, so you casually bring up money conversations. Not specifics, but general talk about stocks, mortgages, your tax advisor, etc. You learn something that you turn around and implement, not knowing that your friend is operating on information he got from someone else who also isn't as financially savvy as appearances would lead you to believe.

Discussing money with others can surely increase your knowledge and improve your financial situation, but the key is to be discussing money with those who know what they're talking about and are in a similar situation. Having spent the last four years working one-on-one with successful individuals who are business owners and business leaders and well respected both in their communities and within their families, I can say with conviction that professional and personal success and intelligence are not indicative of financial success and intelligence. In fact, many of the people in your network whom you'd be most apt to trust based on their success and intelligence and perceived financial savvy don't have their financial affairs in order. Based on this, I never solicit professional advice from anyone except a trusted professional in that field. I might ask for opinions from friends and colleagues, but I never act based on their advice unless I'm 100 percent confident that it's accurate.

> In your answer to the last question, what qualified your past non-professional sources of financial advice to give you that advice? Was it the fact they work at a company that does financial services? Do you know what their role is there? Should you seek advice from them going forward? Why or why not?

Personal and professional success isn't an indicator that someone necessarily has good financial knowledge. Even if someone has good financial knowledge, that person would be hard pressed to give you solid financial advice without having a good grasp on your entire financial picture. I'm guessing you wouldn't be willing to fork over a tax return or investment statements and share your financial goals with the neighbor you chat with about investing in Apple stock.

If you don't have full clarity about where you stand financially and don't know exactly what the best next steps are, you can do one of two things: you can read everything you can about personal finance and take some courses to master the fundamentals so that you're better educated and able to make better financial decisions in light of your situation, or you can hire a professional financial advisor who can help you review your situation and build a plan and offer guidance. What you should never do is implement solicited or unsolicited advice from people who don't have the credentials to actually help you and who are not invested in the outcomes of that advice.

Another thing to remember: Just because your husband/cousin/ uncle "works in finance" doesn't mean he should be your go-to guy for financial questions. Someone who works at Fidelity, for example, could just as easily be managing an IT division or overseeing compliance and have nothing to do with personal finance. In fact, the number of people working in finance at big corporations who actually do financial planning for clients is extremely low. Even if the role is related to personal finance, it's likely that it is in one area, like opening or managing a certain account, instead of managing a client's overall financial picture.

Also note that there are people who say they're financial advisors who only deal with managing investments or selling insurance, and as a result there isn't much financial advice going on. Those people can absolutely give you advice on your portfolio if you tell them what your objective is, but they likely can't help you determine what your optimal portfolio should look like without having an accurate picture of your overall financial situation or a conversation with your financial advisor.

> Have you found yourself buying into or repeating any of these tax-related gripes mentioned above? Did you do any digging to figure out whether it was in fact true for you or your situation?

Likewise they can help you buy an insurance product, but it's impossible for them to know that it's the best fit for you out of every option if they don't know the whole picture. Be careful about whom you're soliciting advice from and whether that person is qualified to give you advice.

* * * * *

One of my biggest pet peeves is hearing misinformed money talk. We've all been privy to it and likely more than once. One of the main financial topics that I hear misinformation around is taxes. Maybe you're even guilty of buying into it or moaning about it yourself. "Taxes are the reason I can't get ahead." "Because I make more money and pay more in taxes, I make less than someone who didn't work as hard and doesn't have a graduate degree." "Oh well, who cares if you had to spend more money on that business expense; it's a write off." I've heard statements along these lines many, many times, in person, on the radio, on television.

I want to point this out is because I've surprisingly heard some very intelligent people say things along these lines. These statements are simply not true, but not only that, if you operate on this misconception and buy into this noise instead of digging deeper, you may miss out on some great opportunities. Taxes are inevitable—you know how the saying goes, "There are only two certainties in life: death and taxes"—but the way you deal with taxes can make them your best friend or your worst enemy.

Education is huge when it comes to your financial situation, whether related to law, taxes, or financial planning. If you haven't figured it out yet, I'm a huge advocate of having a plan for your money, and that doesn't just mean a plan for investing; it also means having a tax plan so that you're able to feel like you have control and clarity over how much money you're able to save in taxes and why you're paying what you pay. This is another example of how working with an expert or developing expert knowledge yourself (if you are willing and able to spend your time that way) is crucial. You absolutely need to educate yourself or pay someone to give you the education you need in order to play an active role in your financial situation.

> What is the first thing that popped into your head when I said "wealthy"? Is wealth a positive or negative thing for you? Do you want to be wealthy?

The biggest mistake you can make is hiring experts to do your financial planning, but not really understanding what they are telling you because you don't know the fundamentals and you aren't committed to dedicating mental capital to your financial situation. If you are hiring someone to either tell you how to fix your problem or to fix it for you, they won't be teaching you everything they know because that's not their role. If you know you have a less than basic understanding of a certain topic, you need to be honest with your advisor and make a decision either to read up or pay for an accelerated catch-up. I can't tell you how many clients have told me that they've worked with people in the past (or even with me) and not understood everything that was being said or done but were too embarrassed to speak up. That's a very dangerous place to be.

Working with a good CPA who knows the ins and outs of tax rules and seeks to understand your specific situation costs more than using TurboTax or hiring a low-cost local accountant, but they'll likely provide thousands of dollars in value by preventing or correcting a mistake or alerting you of opportunities to minimize your tax burden and maximize the money you get to keep in your pocket—which helps you to afford the lifestyle that will make you wealthy on your terms.

If the first thing that popped into your head when you read "wealthy" was being rich or someone you know that is rich, we have some work to do, which we'll get into in the next chapter. For now, I want you to take a few minutes to list your top personal and financial goals. Be very specific. List at least five things that are the most important to you in the world and will give you the lifestyle you dream of. They should be the things you work so hard for. They will be different for you than for your significant other, friends, and family, and that's okay—we're ignoring the noise! For many people, coming up with five goals is hard, but if you have more you can put them in the notes section below. This exercise is only for you and it's extremely important, so be honest and don't worry about what other people would say or think about your answers.

What are your top five personal and financial goals, in order of priority?

1)_____

2)_____

3)_____

4)_____

5)_____

Chapter Questions:

When was the last time you got burned by acting on advice given by someone who wasn't an expert in the field or by hiring a lower-cost service provider? What did you learn from the experience?

_____

_____

_____

_____

When was the last time you looked at the true cost of a bad decision instead of just looking at the price paid? What were the hidden costs?

_____

_____

_____

_____

Who was the last person you took financial advice from that wasn't a professional? Why did you trust that person to give you that advice?

_____

_____

_____

_____

Looking back, are you still confident that they were qualified to give the advice? Why? Is that only based on the advice having worked out for you, or do they actually have background that qualifies them?

_____

_____

_____

_____

In your answer to the last question, what qualified your past non-professional sources of financial advice to give you that advice? Was it the fact they work at a company that does financial services? Do you know what their role is there? Should you seek advice from them going forward? Why or why not?

_____

_____

_____

Have you found yourself buying into or repeating any of these tax-related gripes mentioned above? Did you do any digging to figure out whether it was in fact true for you or your situation?

_____

_____

_____

What is the first thing that popped into your head when I said "wealthy"? Is wealth a positive or negative thing for you? Do you want to be wealthy?

_____

_____

_____

_____

CHAPTER 4

Wealth versus Money

"Wealth is the ability to fully experience life."
—Henry David Thoreau

Amanda is one of the wealthiest people I know—and not because she's managed to amass a big pile of money or properties. Rather, she is very clear about what is important to her and lives life on her terms based on her priorities, which are health and wellness, giving back, family, experiences, and relationships. She is very aware of how her priorities fit in to who she is and who she wants to grow into as a person socially, emotionally, and financially. She is always there for her friends and clients; she's quick to drop a line to say she's thinking about you or to stop by with dinner when you're sick and need a little help. She knows that the money piece is important because she needs to pay her bills and finance her experiences, health and wellness, and giving-back projects, but she is completely unapologetic about living in the moment. She also has no problem saying she can't commit to something that demands either her time or money because she has a bike ride planned or needs to get the morning started walking the dogs with her husband; she knows those are some of her top priorities.

Think of a wealthy individual. Chances are the first person who popped into your head is someone who has an extremely high income and/or net worth—maybe someone like Bill Gates or Richard Branson or even someone you know locally who has been financially successful.

We tend to think about wealth in terms of being rich or having financial assets rather than in terms of the ability to live your best life. You and I both know that money is important to living life on our terms, but I think we overemphasize how important money really is. What I've found is many people actually have the resources to live their best lives, but they're usually not using them as effectively as they could be. One of the main reasons many people fail to fully maximize what their money can do for them is because they don't take the time to sit down and honestly consider what they value in life and what really makes their lives rich.

> Where do you actually spend your money and your time now?
>
> What do your actions say about what you value?

Look back at the list of financial goals and objectives you created at the end of the last chapter. Are those really the things you care most about and work hard for every day? Are they really your most important personal and financial goals? I'm willing to bet that many of the goals on your list are about having the money to achieve something in the distant future. Maybe being able to retire comfortably is on your list. Maybe you have young children and being able to help them with college is one of your goals. But are those things really what are most important to you? I've found that when I ask new clients to do this exercise, most if not all of their goals usually involve saving money for something like retirement and/or their kids' education, but how they're currently spending and saving their money doesn't line up with what they say they want. This suggests that their actions actually aren't aligned with their values or they aren't being honest with themselves (or at least with me) about what really matters to them.

Your personal priorities are yours and only yours. But at the same time, you don't live in a bubble. You live with and interact with other people, and they are often impacted by your decisions just like you're impacted by theirs. If you have a spouse or significant other you share life with, remember that they are their own person with different life experiences and a different view of the world. Their priorities may be completely different than yours, or exactly the same as yours but with a different order or priority, or somewhere in the middle. It is crucial that you don't assume that they are on the same page as you in terms of goals and priority of those goals. You may both think retirement at 65 is non-negotiable, but your spouse may be willing to sacrifice all your other goals to make that retirement happen, whereas you may want to have the mortgage paid off before retiring and be willing to do what it takes now to make that happen.

When you aren't clear on your financial priorities and the order of importance of each, you can't communicate them to someone else and you can't determine whether you are working with each other, in completely opposite directions, or against each other. When we neglect to talk about our priorities and where we stand with our partners, parents, kids, and other loved ones, no one is aware of how their individual actions related to money may actually be unintentionally working against someone else's actions or goals.

This includes your kids. If you've made the decision to not help them with college, be honest with them. Tell them when they start high school so that they are clear on what they need to do if college is a priority for them. They might study a little harder, get a job and save money, or volunteer more so their résumé looks better for scholarship consideration. Also make sure you get them the right resources when it comes to learning about student loans so that they don't make a potentially irreversible and costly mistake when it comes to financing their education.

Again, be honest with yourself and your spouse. If you know you're the kind of parent who will do anything for your kids regardless of how that leaves you financially, don't say you won't help them with college and fail to plan any further, ignoring the reality that there may be other expensive areas you actually will help them in. Be realistic about whether you will help them when the time comes; if you know you won't, then be firm in that decision and don't jeopardize the other goals you have in order to help later on.

Many parents who choose not to pay for college still help their kids in other ways, such as helping to contribute to expenses like room and board, rent, meal plans, and transportation. Those are not normal expenses when your child lives at home and they aren't cheap when the child is in college. Build in a buffer for that stuff and be strict about your limits once you've done an honest assessment and made a decision.

If you're young and single, you also need to be realistic about your priorities. It's easy to neglect planning when you don't have to worry about a spouse or kids, but your planning has implications for your parents and siblings or whoever you would go to for help should you get sick, injured, or laid off. Also be honest about what you really want in life right now. Don't feel pressured to buy a house or condo just because you're an adult and others think that should be a priority. Also don't feel like it's crucial to live on your own when you may be just as happy with roommates. Make decisions about how you want to live and what you want to experience and go after those things instead of letting the opinions of strangers, family, and friends sway you into something that will impact your lifestyle.

The point is that you can't go back and live your life twice. Part of having a wealthy life is the luxury of living life on your own terms, whatever those terms are. Maybe the traditional goals of home ownership, retirement, and adequate emergency savings are your goals. If they are, great! Work towards them. But if those aren't your goals or you'd place them in a different order of priority, don't let guilt or public opinion keep you from going after what you really want.

Time and time again, clients will come to me and say retirement is the top priority. They're usually late to the game, in their late 40s or early 50s, and don't have anywhere near what they need to retire anytime soon—if ever. I might tell them that if they want to have the same lifestyle they have now when they're retired, they need to save $5,000 per month. Why? Because up until now they've been spending almost every single penny they make. They still have a substantial mortgage and can't downsize because they are underwater and still need somewhere to live. They basically have 15 years to save for 30 years of retirement, and they don't have the same leverage they would've had if they'd begun saving regularly much earlier.

Amanda, whom I told you about at the beginning of the chapter, isn't going to save the $5,000 a month. There is no way she can reduce her lifestyle enough to free up this much cash, especially since she has some pretty significant fixed expenses from decisions she's already made. Even if she didn't have those expenses, she is used to the lifestyle that she's had for the last 25 years and isn't going to spend the next 15 eating tuna out of a can just so she can stop working. But she doesn't need to. Planning isn't static and it is an art, not a science. One of the great things about planning is that you can design a strategy that allows you to live a life that fulfills you and makes you feel wealthy so that you wake up every day grateful for who you are and what you have. Sounds a lot better than waking up with the dread of high bills and low savings coupled with an unhealthy fear of the future, doesn't it? Just be sure you are clear about what is and isn't important to you; I do have some clients who feel that having a full retirement is truly non-negotiable.

Let's say Larry and Linda are in a similar situation. After a long talk and some back and forth, they get honest and say that they know they'll never save $5,000 a month—they just aren't willing to reduce their lifestyle to that degree. But they think $3,000 is definitely doable, and they are willing to cut back and do what it takes to get there. They'll be cutting their current lifestyle expenses by $3,000 in order to save, and if they stick to the new lifestyle in retirement, they'll need $36,000 less per year. We leave the meeting with the understanding that the next step is for Larry and Linda to look for $3,000 per month to cut out of their spending and to begin saving that money starting the next month. Six months later, we get back together and they haven't saved a dime. What happened?

It turns out that Larry and Linda's values and priorities are very similar to those of my wealthy friend Amanda. Now, what is someone who lives this kind of lifestyle and who values things like relationships and experiences going to give up? Every single thing they spend money on, with the exception of vacations/getaways, involves other people and is heavily integrated into their lifestyle. They aren't spending money on Starbucks or home décor or clothing. They're spending money on people and experiences that fulfill them and give fulfillment and enjoyment to others. Larry and Linda absolutely need to save, but retirement honestly isn't more important to them than any two or three of these other priorities.

This is why an in-depth assessment of what is truly most important to you is crucial. Larry and Linda should absolutely be able to save that money with no problem. When opportunities arise to give back or to take the trip of a lifetime, they always find the money and make it work because those things are important to them. We always find the money for the things we care most about, and we get it by not spending on the things we care least about. The key is in finding what we actually want.

> What are your lifestyle priorities that you value and that make you feel wealthy and fulfilled?
>
> What have you been saying are your top financial priorities in the past exercises? Are these actually your priorities? Why or why not?

You might assume that I'm going to say that Larry and Linda don't love each other or their kids if they don't start saving for retirement, but you'd be wrong. Yes, if they don't work to come up with a plan they can get on board with and start saving *something*, then I'll say that they're acting like they don't love their family, but one of the greatest things about planning is that it's customized.

No one can tell you that you need to save for retirement portfolio income if you're willing to give up some security and instead invest in real estate or a business that will give passive income or work as a consultant part-time in retirement. For Larry and Linda, the latter options would actually fulfill their social needs and provide a platform for ongoing opportunities to give back. So as long as they've put the proper plan in place so that this decision doesn't negatively impact the other spouse, kids, or parents in the event of death, disability, divorce, or other dramatic life events, it is something they can consider.

The conventional wisdom we're battling here is that building wealth means building assets. Conventional wisdom says you need to work towards getting a better job to make more money, paying off your house to have equity, and having a substantial retirement account and other savings in order to be wealthy. And we take it a step further by being so obsessed with percentages and arbitrary numbers: "You need to put 20 percent of your income towards financial priorities." "You should put 10 percent of your income towards retirement." "A million dollars is the magic amount for retirement." This information falls way short because it doesn't take into consideration how old you are, who you are, how much you make, and, most importantly, what you want in life.

Have you been saving according to rules of thumb? Has it worked or has it tripped you up? Have you neglected to save because you feel the benchmark is too high, or because the goal you're "supposed" to be working towards doesn't resonate? If that's the case, what is the potential impact of your lack of planning on those you love? What does resonate with you that you feel confident you can commit to working towards?

> What are your true priorities, and what are the new goals you are working towards now that you've identified these priorities? How do these goals fit in with how you see your current and future selves financially, socially, emotionally, and physically?

If it turns out that some of the goals you've been working towards actually *are* high on your priority list, that's great. Have you been systematically trying to achieve them, and are you positive you're effectively leveraging your resources? Are you clear on exactly how close or far you are from actually accomplishing it? If not, it could be because even though you're aware of what you want and need you haven't gotten specific enough.

After people come to a realization that what they thought were priorities truly aren't important, they need to dig down deep and get as specific as possible about what they do want. When I said that the hypothetical couple earlier in the chapter needed to save $5,000 and then $3,000 to get the retirement lifestyle they said they wanted, the only way I could come up with those figures is by getting the couple to identify how much after-tax income they needed per month in retirement and what age they were comfortable retiring at.

In reassessing and deciding what's important to you, you always need to put a realistic dollar amount on your goals. If your number one priority is being able to go on vacation every year and pay cash for it, you need to identify whether your desired vacation costs $1,000 or $10,000. Is it visiting a national park every year and camping, or is it eating and drinking your way through a European country every year? The same goes for helping your kids. Does giving them their first car mean they get yours and you need the money to buy a new one that's in the $40,000 range, or does it mean giving them a few thousand dollars for a clunker? To effectively plan and create leverage in your life and have the lifestyle that makes you wealthy on your terms, you need to establish your true goals and priorities, put a dollar amount on them, and reverse engineer how to get there.

Chapter Questions:

Where do you actually spend your money and your time now? What do your actions say about what you value?

_____

_____

_____

_____

What are your lifestyle priorities that you value and that make you feel wealthy and fulfilled?

_____

_____

_____

_____

What have you been saying are your top financial priorities in the past exercises? Are these actually your priorities? Why or why not?

_____

_____

_____

_____

Have you been saving according to rules of thumb? Has it worked or has it tripped you up?

_____

_____

_____

_____

Have you neglected to save because you feel the benchmark is too high, or because the goal you're "supposed" to be working towards doesn't resonate? If that's the case, what is the potential impact of your lack of planning on those you love? What does resonate with you that you feel confident you can commit to working towards?

_____

_____

_____

_____

What are your true priorities, and what are the new goals you are working towards now that you've identified these priorities? How do these goals fit in with how you see your current and future selves financially, socially, emotionally, and physically?

_____

_____

_____

_____

Put dollar amounts on the true goals and priorities you established in the last exercise.

_____

_____

_____

_____

CHAPTER 5

Save Smarter, Not Harder

"There are no secrets to success. It is the result of preparation,
hard work, and learning from failure."
—Colin Powell

We see it on the news and in the paper on a daily basis. Americans are constantly approaching their finances with a reactive, not proactive, mindset. The consequences can be dire. Much of the time, the impact of a life circumstance that is being reacted to could have been significantly reduced had some proactive planning been done. The right amount of disability insurance could have prevented someone from losing their house and being dependent on family and friends—or worse, on the street. Likewise, an adequate emergency fund could have prevented significant credit card debt that led to huge monthly interest payments and an inability to save for retirement. Paying for good legal advice instead of asking a family member or colleague could have prevented a loss of assets or filing for bankruptcy, which minimizes options to leverage your future dollars.

Especially in the realm of financing education, many Americans are actually saving harder, not smarter. I'd be willing to bet you fall into this category, which means you aren't leveraging your dollars to maximize their buying power. I'm sure you've made financial mistakes around paying for education, either your own or a child's. You either took out too many loans, took out the wrong loans, didn't save enough, or saved the wrong way. But whether you're a future parent, a parent with kids who aren't in college yet, a grandparent with grandkids that you intend to help with their education, or even a parent who has kids already in college and wants to help them out, you still have time to turn the tide or at least minimize the blow your decision will have on your financial situation.

The chances are pretty good that you, or someone you know, have at least one student loan, maybe from your own education or a child's. If you don't, you may be facing a decision of whether to take one on. If you do, you're not alone: 40 million Americans have student loan debt[9], and I hear all the time in my office, on the news, and in conversation that this debt can be financially crippling. When the amount you're required to pay on your student loan each month can be equivalent to a small mortgage payment, it's hard to build a good financial foundation. So why do so many Americans take on this level of debt? Because mistakes were likely made along the way and the money to pay for education up front likely wasn't there, yet many people can agree that education is one of the most important tools today.

In fact, 89 percent of parents value education as an investment in their children's financial future, according to a study done by Ipsos,[10] the global research company. The study notes that most parents are so confident in the success of a college education that 80 percent are willing to stretch themselves financially to save for college. This may explain how we got to this place of Americans owing a combined 1.2 trillion dollars in federal student loan debt alone, but it doesn't answer the question of why 80 percent of Americans say they are willing to stretch themselves financially to pay for education yet only about 50 percent of American families are actually saving for it.

There are really two things to address here. First, we just established that nearly 9 out of 10 Americans think education is an investment in their children's futures, but only about half of them actually save for it. We all know that many people will do whatever they can to help their kids, especially if the help is an investment in their future success, but

---

9   Experian, September 9, 2014, " Experian analysis finds student loans increased by 84 percent since the recession; 40 million consumers now have at least one student loan" www.experianplc.com/media/news/2014

10   Sallie Mae, "How America Saves For College 2015" http://news.salliemae.com/research-tools/america-saves-2015

these statistics show that they'll be doing it the hard way and not the smart way. The problem with the hard way in many cases is that it makes it nearly impossible to actually get the results you want. So your intentions are good, you're going to work hard, but at the end of the day it's not enough because you drain your retirement savings or the equity from your house, or your kids end up saddled with student loan debt anyway, which will impact their ability to have a success story with their own kids.

There are some common reasons people give for why they aren't saving for college, with the top one being they don't have enough money. In my experience, many of the people who say they don't have enough money really should be honest and say they don't care enough about their child's future to do it. As you read this you may be thinking to yourself, "Nicky, you don't know what you're talking about! I love my kids and I'd love to help them with college, but I really don't have enough money! It's hard just getting by!" Then answer these questions honestly:

1) Have you gone on vacation in the past year?

2) Do you go out to eat or order takeout a few times per month?

3) Do you have more than basic cable?

4) Do you have a personal smartphone? Is it less than two years old?

5) Do you buy Christmas gifts every year?

For every yes answer, write down how much you think that item costs over the course of a year. Every single year.

Many people who say they are barely getting by can answer yes to at least one of these questions and usually several, if not all. Every single one of those things is a luxury, not a necessity. Don't get me wrong—I can answer yes to every single one of those questions too, but I know that none of them are necessities and every single one could be cut out if I needed to. I need a phone for business, but I don't need the newest iPhone. I need to eat three meals per day, but I don't need to have a sit-down lunch or dinner out or order delivery, which costs more than preparing something at home and requires extra charges for service. I might need a break from working so hard and have paid vacation I can use, but there are things that can be done locally that don't require a plane ticket, hotel room, meals out, or expensive excursions. Life is all about choices, and part of saving smart is figuring out what non-necessities you really enjoy and are really important to your family and cutting out the less-important things that we usually spend money on without even thinking about how much we actually enjoy them.

Funny enough, I just had someone in my office who actually could say no to those 5 questions. She'd heard me being interviewed on the radio, went to my website, and wrote me the following message:

"Hi Nicole I need help with financial advice please. The more money I make the poorer I get. I don't make a lot of money like the typical hard working individual, but I currently make $45,000 as of January of this year. My bills are somewhat the same amount from when I was making $30,000-35,000, but I still have a hard time saving money. Please help me!"

Now, to be honest, I didn't know anything else about this woman's situation initially. She could have been a single mom working hard to support her family, but struggling or she could have been married to someone whose salary covered all their expenses and she could have just been blowing all her money. I had no idea, so I called her to schedule an appointment. When she came in it turned out that she wasn't single, but that she did have a son and her husband was active duty in the military living out of state. Although he helped with the rent and some utilities, their son's daycare, which she was responsible for was about 50 percent of her monthly income, she was giving 10 percent of her income to her church every week for tithes, and the other 40 percent was going to basic cable and internet, a minimal cellphone plan, groceries, a life insurance policy, and her credit card payment. After all was said and done she had about $300 per month or $75 left per week for anything discretionary (including gas or subway pass to get to and from work and school) and that was if she cut back on grocery costs, and right now everything was being spent. I told her I could understand why it was so tough for her to save because I could imagine things came up all the time having not only herself but a son to worry about, and she told me "I order things online all the time $20 here $50 there and it's stuff that I don't need. I know there is money there to save, I just need help controlling my spending." I was floored. I've sat down with people who make literally ten times what this woman makes and will make every excuse about why they haven't started saving for retirement and can't put money in an emergency fund or find money to invest and here was someone with who many people wouldn't argue with if she said she didn't have any money, and she was taking personal responsibility and not making any excuses for herself. Unless you live below the poverty line, there is always money for something extra. That extra can be saved or it can be spent, it's up to you: it's about priorities.

> Can you relate to this scenario? Did you grow up with parents like this or are you working hard to raise kids and dealing with a similar balancing act? How is trying to give your kids everything now jeopardizing your ability to save for their futures? What things do you give your kids now that are costing them future security?

Now that I've illustrated how the number one excuse usually doesn't hold up, let's look at a pretty common real-life example of someone who falls into the 50 percent of parents who don't save[11] and are doing things the hard way: a former classmate of mine named Joe. You probably have a friend or colleague just like him. You might even be him. Joe loves his kids, Jack and Jane, so much that he works hard every day at work to give them the best lives possible. He works overtime to maximize his income and be the prime candidate for promotions. When he comes home he's tired, but he always makes time to throw the football around with Jack and paint with Jane.

When Joe thinks back to his childhood, he has great memories of summers at the beach with his parents: they weren't rich but they always made sure to spend time together on vacation. Joe makes more than his parents did and wants to give his kids the best he can, so every summer he takes Jack, Jane, and his wife, Jenny, on a trip to Disney World. Every Christmas, he goes all out; this year he's even getting the kids an iPad to share as one of their gifts. Joe doesn't have much in savings and what he does have will likely go towards the credit card bill after the vacation or

11   Sallie Mae, "How America Saves For College 2015" http://news.salliemae.com/research-tools/america-saves-2015

after Christmas. He has a small retirement account from an old job that he only opened because there was a company match at the time, and he hasn't gotten around to opening college savings accounts for the kids yet because he just doesn't know where the money is going to come from. He's thought about their education, but because he can only commit to $50 per month each, he'd rather just put it in savings accounts for the kids. That way, if they need something else, the money is there.

Typical scenario, right? Now let's fast-forward 12 years to Jack's senior year of high school. Joe can't even believe how time has flown! His son is almost an adult, and has been accepted to all five schools he's applied to, both public and private schools. Joe had saved almost $8,000 in the savings account he started for Jack, but he used more than half of that to get Jack a car when he got his license. Joe and Jenny let Jack know that if he wants to go to a public school they will help him with the tuition and fees (if he stays in state and lives at home to keep costs down), but that if he wants to go to one of the private schools he got into he will have to take out student loans.

Jack wants to be a marine biologist and there is a fantastic program he got into at a private university in Florida. It will cost about $50,000 per year, but he knows that if he doesn't take the opportunity and goes to a public school with a less-renowned program he won't be able to get a job in his field at graduation, so he takes the student loans out in order to attend the school in Florida. Joe and Jenny want to help their son, so they agree to use the $10,000 per year they would have shelled out on public school tuition to help him with room and board. They intend to pay this however they can—out of income by cutting back on expenses, out of savings, and even out of their retirement accounts. Joe and Jenny are proud that their son got into that program, and that he was able to take out student loans to cover the costs, but they are nervous that when he graduates he will have to move back home because he won't be able to afford his student loan payments and an apartment on his own with the income from his first job. They're also beginning to stress out about the fact that Jane will be in college in two years and they know they will have to help her as well.

If a parent spends all the money he makes taking the kids to Disney every summer and buying them great presents every Christmas, does that make him a great parent? If when the kids get to college, their only option is to take on student loan debt or compromise their education, does that parent love their kids? My instinct is to say no, but I know exactly what you're thinking: "Of course they love their kids! Saving is hard and they did the best they could."

I know Joe and Jenny love their kids, but in situations like these it's my firm belief that they aren't acting like it—and they're definitely not saving like it. I know saving is hard, but it's also hard trying to scrape together money, getting into debt, and making severe lifestyle compromises to help their kids after failing to plan.

Joe and Jenny could have saved $250 per month starting from the time Jack was born. Had they put this money in their savings account (which doesn't get any interest), but the time Jack turned 18 they'd have saved $54,000. Had they saved the same amount of money into a college savings plan where they could take advantage of the combination of compound interest, tax deferred growth, and market returns, the same savings could have provided Jack with $102,000 at age 18. Almost double the money! This is assuming an expected yearly average market returns of 6 percent (which isn't very aggressive considering historical average returns of the S&P500).

So instead of having to scramble to somehow find a way to obtain the $54,000 per year the family estimates needing down the road to be able to send Jack to the private University they both went to in order to cover the four years of in-state tuition or the room and board, the family could have planned in advance and gotten more for their dollars. It's the same $54,000 saved, but the account and the amount of time invested for growth matters. If Joe and Jenny still chose to help Jack with room and board down the road in addition to the $100,000 saved, they could have saved their son well over that amount in student loan payments, which could be the difference between him being able to buy a condo as a young college grad or needing to live at home.

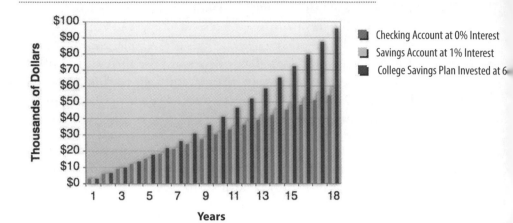

College Plan is illustrated at 6% while the Checking Account is illustrated at 0%. This is a hypothetical example and is not representative of any specific situation. Your results will vary. The hypothetical rates of return used do not reflect the deduction of fees and charges inherent to investing. Investing in a college plan involves risk, including loss of principal

As Joe and Jenny's story shows us, not saving smart has an extremely high cost even just financially. There are also ancillary costs, because failing to save smart often means becoming a burden on those we love by requiring their time, money, or both. (Do you know anyone who has a family member or friend living with them out of necessity, someone who, due to sickness, injury, death of a caretaker, divorce, or financial hardship can't take care of themselves?)

Saving smarter is all about choices. Disney every year might be non-negotiable for your family, but $250 per month could just as easily be the cable package. Many families I meet with barely have time to even watch TV. With work and school schedules, sports, hobbies, and social commitments, it's easy to feel like you're only home to eat and sleep, but many people would never dream of giving up their cable package. What is more important: cable or college? Maybe the answer is cable, and if it is, that's up to you.

> Be honest with yourself right now: If you have kids or grandkids that you'd like to help with college, are you currently saving every month for them? If you aren't, why aren't you?
>
> What is more important than investing in that child's future? If you are saving, are you saving enough and are you saving according to a plan?

Take this a step further: Your main priority might not be saving for a child's education, but what is your top financial priority or goal? Is there anything you know you can immediately cut out that would generate the monthly savings required to achieve one or more of the goals outlined above?

Before I move on to addressing the other half of the issue, which is people who save but don't save smart, I want to take a minute to remind you to ignore the noise. Part of the benefit of having a plan for your savings—whether for college, retirement, or another goal—is that as long as you're finding a way to save the money necessary to accomplish that goal, it doesn't matter how you spend the rest of your money. Saving according to a plan also means you have to save less of your hard-earned money because a clear plan allows you to utilize strategies and accounts that give you leverage, either through tax deferral, investments, or tax deductions.

What does this have to do with ignoring the noise? You just made a decision in the exercise above to give up some things and keep others in order to have the cash flow to save for your most important goals. You might be willing to give up driving into work and paying for parking and choose to take public transportation instead in order to free up some cash. Or you might decide to give up your morning Starbucks, weekend dinners out, or weekday takeout in order to keep the family vacations and fund your expensive retail habit.

The point is, as long as you find the money somewhere, don't let other people who weren't part of your decision process and who don't live your life make you feel guilty for your spending choices or try to advise you to make different choices. If always having a new car is what you love and choose to spend your money on, don't let someone tell you a lease is a waste of money or a bad idea. It's your decision to spend your discretionary income the way you want—as long as you're saving for your financial priorities according to a plan and creating leverage in your life.

Now, even though this concept of saving smarter, not harder is widely applicable across different segments of your financial life, I'm going to stay with the topic of college education funding because many can agree on the importance of education. We already talked about the 48 percent of American parents who are saving harder, not smarter because they aren't saving for college at all and they, along with their children, will have to pay the cost of those decisions later. Now, let's talk about those who are saving but just aren't saving smart.

Often, people will think that they are saving smart because they're investing in the market or they are saving in vehicles specific to their goals, but they are looking at savings the wrong way. The smart way to save is to start by protecting what you have (car insurance protects against the cost of car accidents, health insurance prevents the burden of sky-high medical bills, disability insurance replaces your paycheck if you're out of work for a specific amount of time). Then, move on to saving to prevent your goals being sabotaged (an emergency fund so you don't have to accumulate credit card debt, or a plan to aggressively pay down debt). The final step is leveraging what you've saved by investing in different markets (stock market, real estate, commodities) and in different vehicles.

Sometimes these three steps can happen simultaneously, as part of a save-smart strategy. These steps should never happen in the reverse order, but that is how many people learn to save. People today are required to have health insurance, homeowners insurance (if they have a mortgage), and car insurance (if they have a car), so some of the protection is taken care of. But there is no law mandating life insurance to protect your mortgage or your family's standard of living, disability insurance to protect your paycheck, long-term care insurance to protect against the high cost of nursing homes, or umbrella insurance to protect against liability claims if someone sues you.

Did you realize that there was such a high cost associated with not saving in the right vehicles? Do you feel like you're not using your resources adequately now that you know the power of saving smart? In what areas could you save smarter?

All of those should be top priority—in differing degrees depending on your circumstances—because they immediately create leverage and protect against things that can so easily blow up your plan. Instead, people are almost obsessed with the stock market and investing. All they hear about is the S&P and the Dow or how lucrative real estate is and how many success stories have come out of a great stock pick or business investment or real estate move.

We save backwards constantly, perhaps because the stock market seems sexier than insurance. Someone who has $1,000 to their name in a savings account is far more likely to invest in the stock market than use the money as the building blocks of an emergency fund or to get insurance to protect future earnings. And then life happens, and maybe that person loses their job. The 200 percent return they got on that $1,000 has nowhere near the same impact on their immediate situation and their future as continuing to receive most of their paycheck would have. America has to stop worrying about investing first, saving second, and protection last (if at all). If people spending more than they make is America's top problem, then a lack of financial foundation and strategic savings is problem number two.

You might think that those who are diligently saving are likely utilizing the tools available to stretch their dollars furthest, especially because of the vast amount of information and advice out there related to savings and investments, but the truth is the vast majority aren't. According to a report done by the country's largest private student-loan lender, Sallie Mae, and Ipsos, only 48 percent of American parents with children under 18 are actually saving for college. They also found that 69 percent of them are putting those savings into checking accounts and general savings accounts. They're making the effort to save, but they're putting that hard-earned money into accounts that don't even keep pace with inflation. The graph from Joe and Jenny's example earlier in this chapter shows how big the difference is even when the investments are only moderate and not aggressive.

There are two issues with general savings being earmarked for college savings (and this argument holds strong with regard to retirement savings as well). The first is that when you're saving for a specific goal, there are certain strategies and vehicles that can be leveraged to grow your savings much more significantly. But by not saving smart, you are foregoing that leverage. I strongly believe that parents have an obligation to do the best they can for their kids and to get educated and act accordingly so that they can teach their kids basic life skills around money both directly and through their actions. As a parent, knowing there are vehicles out there (like 529 plans, for example) that can enhance the savings for your child's future and not using them could be perceived as negligent. Even having an adequate basic savings account as an emergency fund that would prevent the necessity to use debt in case of emergency could significantly increase your future savings both in the short and the long run.

The second problem with earmarking general savings for college is that many Americans, whether they're savers or not, have bad money behaviors, and having all your savings in one place makes it way too easy to slip into those behaviors. There aren't any statistics on how many of the 69 percent who use checking and savings accounts for college savings don't actually use all of that money for what it was originally intended for, but I have a hunch the number is pretty high.

Bad money behaviors often involve a lack of discipline and are commonly associated with a lack of saving. In other words, people don't save because if they see the money in their bank account, they find it hard not to spend it. Even those who do save have bad money behaviors that limit their ability to achieve their savings goals. Many savers know what they're saving for—college funding, retirement, a rainy day fund, vacations—but they don't have a very clear vision of what those things cost and how all the pieces fit into place in light of their lives and lifestyle. So a saver might actually have the discipline to accumulate that $54,000 or maybe even $154,000 in their savings account ; however, when it comes time to spend the money that's accumulated, they find there are many competing goals and that there isn't enough to go around.

For example, Joe could be saving diligently for Jack's college instead of spending everything he makes. If he keeps that money in a savings account and not specifically a college fund, however, it is all too easy to tap into that savings to pay for Jack's first car, or a senior class trip to Costa Rica, or any number of other things unrelated to Jack but important to the family's livelihood. If Jenny loses her job, it's much easier for the family to use the college savings to maintain the lifestyle instead of making big sacrifices to reduce their lifestyle.

The bottom line is that studies show time and time again that most people are spenders, not savers, and in my experience bad habits usually win over good intentions. So when you leave all your savings in a general savings account, there are issues with double counting savings for multiple goals and having to decide what is top priority at the end of the road. And if we're honest, you'd probably agree that many people wouldn't ever make it to the savings goal without needing to tap into the money for more immediately pressing expenses. Because let's face it—life happens.

Saving smarter is also about understanding your financial situation. Maybe you're a good saver: you're able to max out your 401(k) every year, are putting 10 percent per year towards retirement and another 10 percent per year towards other financial priorities. You might think based on what you hear from the talking heads on TV or personal finance magazines and books that you're doing a great job and are well on your way to financial freedom, but you'd be wrong. Because if you're disciplined enough to save for retirement but retirement isn't a core priority for you, when the time comes to travel, help family or friends, or buy a new car, you'll likely pay a penalty and taxes to make a withdrawal from your retirement account, which may negate the interest you earned and give you less than you'd have had if you put that money in a different vehicle.

Just as easily, you could accumulate a three to six month emergency fund, which is what many money gurus will tell you is more than adequate, and put the rest of your money in other vehicles like CDs, stocks, bonds, retirement accounts, or college plans—but you could lose your job, have a bad tenant, or hit some other rough patch, and all of a sudden the cost of simply saving according to general percentages leaves you worse than had you just kept all of your money in a basic savings account. That's why understanding your situation and making decisions that are customized to your goals, needs, and lifestyle is so crucial.

We're going to move on to talk about what many Americans regard as their biggest investment: their home. But first, I want you to reflect a bit about where you fit in with the smarter versus harder debate.

Chapter Questions:

Would you classify yourself as someone who usually saves hard or smart when it comes to your finances? Why or why not? Are you failing to save or failing to leverage? Or are you great at one but not the other?

_____

_____

_____

_____

Is this who you want to be? Why or why not? Where can you improve?

_____

_____

_____

_____

Saving smarter means saving according to a plan, which means doing everything strategically in light of your goals and objectives. Goals and objectives shouldn't only be financial. How do you see yourself socially, emotionally, and financially, both now and in the future when those goals are reached?

_____

_____

_____

_____

Can you relate to Joe's scenario earlier in the chapter? Did you grow up with parents like this or are you working hard to raise kids and dealing with a similar balancing act? How is trying to give your kids everything now jeopardizing your ability to save for their futures? What things do you give your kids now that are costing them future security?

_____

_____

_____

_____

Be honest with yourself right now: If you have kids or grandkids that you'd like to help with college, are you currently saving every month for them? If you aren't, why aren't you? What is more important than investing in that child's future? If you are saving, are you saving enough and are you saving according to a plan?

_____

_____

_____

_____

Take this a step further: Your main priority might not be saving for a child's education, but what is your top financial priority or goal? Write it down and put a star next to it, and feel free to add a few secondary goals as well. Be specific!

_____

_____

_____

_____

Make a list. What can you cut out that would generate the monthly savings required to achieve one or more of the goals outlined above?

_____

_____

_____

_____

Did you realize that there was such a high cost associated with not saving in the right vehicles? Do you feel like you're not using your resources adequately now that you know the power of saving smart? In what areas could you save smarter?

_____

_____

_____

_____

CHAPTER 6

The Real Estate Myth

"Many novice real estate investors soon quit the profession and invest in a well-diversified portfolio of bonds. That's because, when you invest in real estate, you often see a side of humanity that stocks, bonds, mutual funds, and saving money shelter you from."
—Robert Kiyosaki

When Mark and Mary first started out, they were renting a studio apartment in the city that cost them far too much, but was convenient for getting to work and meeting up with friends. They got married and a few years later Mary got pregnant with their son, Mikey. The realization of how expensive babies are prompted them to look for a cheaper apartment in the suburbs, but they wound up deciding on a two-bedroom townhouse for the same price instead. They figured they needed the space because Mikey would need his own room before too long, and they were already used to paying that rent anyway. Then came Maggie. Mark knew that it would be a while before the kids needed their own rooms, but he began thinking about how the development that their townhouse was in wasn't the best environment for their kids to grow up in. It wasn't dangerous, but there were no other young families in the neighborhood and there was no backyard for the kids to play outside. The development also didn't allow animals, and he and Mary wanted the kids to grow up with a dog.

So they started house hunting. Family and friends were so excited for the couple. They were excited too. They continually heard people make comments about how it was "better to pay your own mortgage and own something than to throw away money paying someone else's" and that "a home is an investment" and "property *always* appreciates." They'd always heard homeownership was a good financial decision and they were happy that being so smart financially was going to give their kids the childhood the couple had envisioned. They shopped around and ended up paying a few hundred dollars more on their mortgage than they'd been paying on rent, but hey, Mark had recently gotten a promotion and they were willing to stretch themselves a bit to get a home with the layout they'd envisioned in a vibrant neighborhood.

Fast-forward five years. The couple now has four young kids; space is tight and their home no longer fits their situation so they are thinking of moving. They want to live in a town with a better school district because they've recently found out that Maggie has learning disabilities. They need not just a bigger house but one that is more updated because their starter home, while affordable, became a money pit. They've had trouble saving diligently over these past years because their family has almost doubled in size and ever since they bought the house it seems like there is always something to pay for, either in upgrades or unexpected maintenance.

They meet with a realtor to figure out where they stand in terms of selling their first home to buy their second. It turns out that the couple's home did increase in value, but because only a small portion of their mortgage payments went to principal and the rest went to interest, property taxes, PMI, and homeowners insurance, they still owe almost as much as they originally purchased it for. Plus, after commissions and other costs associated with purchasing a new home, they will basically be starting out at square one all over again. All the money they paid into the mortgage didn't result in any equity that they could use towards the purchase of their new home, and they have spent thousands of dollars more on replacing the boiler and other appliances, fixing a rotting deck, and so on.

Mark and Mary were actually lucky. Even though they didn't have much to show for their first purchase, they were able to give their kids a yard and a dog and have the lifestyle they wanted. Their first home wasn't a great investment, but they were okay with it because it provided other benefits. And by moving to their second home when they did, they missed the market crash. Had they waited a few more years to upgrade they wouldn't have been able to, because their first home would have ended up being worth less than what they owed. They would have been trapped like so many other families who were hurt by the timing and didn't have the savings or resources to get out at a loss even if they wanted to.

> If you're thinking about buying a new home or property, is it for financial/investment reasons or quality-of-life reasons? If financial reasons, how can you determine the actual estimated return, taking risk into consideration, to know if this is really a good investment? If they're quality-of-life reasons, what are you willing to give up to offset this expense so that you are still able to save?

Real estate essentially comes down to timing, both in the market and in life. So many of my friends want to buy homes right now because they feel like they're throwing away money renting, but they are still in transition and don't even realize it. They may be able to get a good deal on a condo or starter home right now because the market is still low, but they are working their first jobs out of college and have no idea what the short-term future holds. They're not planning on staying in their current jobs forever and they are very aware that they will be on the job hunt in the next few years, but they realistically don't know where that job hunt might take them—possibly a different city, but also quite possibly a different state or country.

If they bought in a good location with good demand and high rents, then moving to a different city would be no problem. Best-case scenario, renting out that property would cover the mortgage and other expenses and add a few hundred dollars a month to their bottom line. Worst-case scenario, they end up with bad tenants who don't pay, but likely they'll do their due diligence and will be able to price out low-quality tenants because of location and demand. Reality will fall somewhere in the middle and they'll be able to rent another place to live closer to work, but still have the ability to be an active landlord and check in on their property.

If they bought in a location that was affordable but not convenient to public transportation or the expressway, where rents are low, and there is more supply than demand, moving to another city could be very costly. It may be hard to cover the mortgage and expenses, and it's likely that they'd end up paying more between their rent and their homeowner-related expenses. It may still be doable, but in this case it's clear that the return on investment is low or potentially negative if they have higher expenses due to high tenant turnover or tenant damage and wear and tear.

> Are you a homeowner who purchased a house as an investment and it turned out not to be? What would you do differently next time? Or if it turned out to be a great investment, how do you know it's a great investment—by running the numbers or some other way?

Either way, if they buy looking at even their primary residence as an investment they may do okay if life changes and they stay in close proximity, but what happens if a great opportunity calls them to move across the country or to a different country? If they sell in a short time frame they likely will break even or sell at a loss if it's a single-family home or a condo. If they keep it and rent it out, they now have the additional expense of needing to hire someone to act as landlord and take care of things while they're gone. It's a tough space to be in.

It is not necessarily a bad investment for a single-family property to be your primary residence. But keep in mind that times have changed. Instead of buying a home that they will live in forever, many Americans are very mobile and move several times, which typically negatively impacts the return on the real estate they buy and sell. I'm also saying that the conventional wisdom that real estate is *always* a good idea is wrong.

Today, we need to be strategic about any real estate purchase and be aware of whether we're looking at it as an investment or whether it isn't an investment but something that is important to our happiness. Buying the most expensive house in the neighborhood is almost never a good idea, but if that's the house you love and want to raise your family in, and you understand that when you go to sell it you likely won't be able to get much more than what you paid for it and you don't care, then buy it. But don't look at that as an investment, and don't feel guilty about it if that's the case. People buy things all the time that don't make them money but give them some other kind of satisfaction. Just because others think your real estate should be an investment doesn't mean it actually needs to be. Just make sure you are aware of whether it is or isn't, because I've seen many clients get an unpleasant surprise when what they thought was an asset has turned out to be a liability because of the economic environment or the timing of life choices.

> Have you decided to invest in real estate in the past, or is it something you've been thinking about lately? Why or why not? What would you want it to provide for you or what has it provided already?

Now that we've gotten the "single family/primary residence is always an investment" myth out of the way, let's talk about something I'm extremely passionate about: real estate investing. I'm talking about true real estate investing—purchasing multi-family properties, flipping houses, or making strategic purchasing decisions based on expected return. I mentioned in an earlier chapter that I own an investment property. That property also happens to be my primary residence.

I decided a few years ago that because of the unstable nature of being self-employed, I needed some passive income. I realized that the market was at a low at the time and people just weren't buying. I wasn't actively looking at that time, but I'd casually browse listings online and see that houses were sitting on the market and I knew I wanted to buy. Part of the reason I wanted to buy is that I was living in a city right outside of Boston and rents were ridiculously high and climbing. I'd rented there for three years and after crunching numbers I saw a huge opportunity in being a landlord.

I finally decided to seriously shop around for houses. I wanted a two- or three-family house in a great location with minimal work to be done, but nothing that fit that description was in my price range in the city I wanted and was familiar with, so I had to make some concessions. I did find a multi-family in a great location, but there was more work to be done than I wanted, especially since I'm not handy at all. I also had never bought a home before and the realtor I ended up using didn't help guide me through the negotiations process so I ended up paying full asking price for the house, which I realized immediately after was much higher than I should have offered and paid.

I definitely made mistakes along the way, but they all worked out. I was adamant about the rents I wanted from the property. I was confident these prices were supported by the location, updates I made, and the market, even though the realtor I hired to handle the rentals was skeptical. I ended up getting a higher-than-average rental income from the first unit I rented and took my time to make subsequent updates to the rest of the house. Two years later, the property is worth at least $100,000 more than what I paid for it, not because of renovations, but because the market has rebounded substantially in this area and supply is low on multi-family properties. I've been told that the renovations will definitely contribute to the value down the line, which is nice, but I made the improvements for personal enjoyment and not for a greater return on investment.

> When it comes to investing, in real estate or otherwise, do you find yourself more comfortable sticking to one kind of investment that you've had success with in the past rather than diversifying? Why? What intimidates you about diversifying?

Purchasing a multi-family home with no spouse and no kids also gave me pretty significant flexibility to choose to have roommates or not. Over the years I've had several roommates who have paid rent and helped offset the cost of my utilities, which created an additional income stream and helped to fund the home improvements I needed to make to enjoy my unit. Aside from the financial benefits, I've also been able to help out my siblings and family members as well.

Real estate shouldn't be your only investment, but I absolutely believe that it's a crucial part of your portfolio both for diversification (because it's not directly correlated to the stock market) and for tax reasons. Many people who've had success with real estate in the past find it easy to fall in love with the passive income and strong returns, and these people usually want to invest in real estate at the expense of investing in other areas. One piece of conventional wisdom I do believe in when it comes to finance is not to put all your eggs in one basket; this rings just as true for real estate investing as it does for stock market investing.

When it comes to investing in the stock market, you've probably heard the disclaimer "past performance is not an indication of future results." Which is a fancy way of saying just because something has been a good investment in the past doesn't mean it will be a good investment in the future. The same holds true for real estate. I've had great tenants in the past and the value of my property has gone up, but that doesn't mean that my next batch of tenants won't be a nightmare or that my next property won't decline in value shortly after I buy it.

> Have you ever felt that there was a compelling reason for you to keep all of your eggs in one basket despite being cautioned on the risk? That the answer is so obvious because it has served you so well before? In what area are you not diversifying, and what are you doing elsewhere in your life to minimize the risk this brings? If nothing, pick a way to diversify to add a layer of risk management.

There is risk associated with all investments, but there is also the potential for higher returns. Even putting money in the bank has some degree of risk associated with it, as we know from the bank failures in the 1920s and 1930s. Many of us know that only $250,000 of deposits are covered by the FDIC should a bank default. Many people today also don't have $250,000 in bank deposits, so we view money in the bank as risk-free. What I've noticed is that even though many of us intellectually understand that there is risk associated with investing in our businesses, real estate, and the stock market, the more success one has in any of these areas the more likely that person is to feel that there is lower risk associated with investing in that area. It's a false sense of security that has some very real implications.

Let's pretend for a moment that I bought two more houses for a total of three properties. All of them are worth over $100,000 more than I paid for them and all of them have great tenants who pay high rents on time and respect my properties. My net worth is pretty high right now, I have strong equity, and I'm excited to continue investing in property. I'm a great saver who saves about 25 percent of my income for my financial priorities, but right now my main priority is to keep investing my savings into real estate. I'm only 26; I can open up a retirement account and build up an emergency fund in my savings account later. Besides, if there's an emergency I can just take money out of the equity in one of the houses by opening a Home Equity Line of Credit.

The unfortunate thing about investing is that timing is a key component. I'm not talking about market timing, like knowing what to buy and sell when. I'm talking about environmental timing. Life timing. The unfortunate thing about investing is that so often, all of your returns are on paper. You don't actually get to realize the returns until you sell. The unfortunate thing about selling is that there are costs associated, such as transaction fees and/or taxes, and once you sell you forfeit the potential for that investment to keep growing. It's a catch 22.

Let's turn back to my hypothetical situation with the three properties. At the time when my real estate was great, I didn't need the money and had no interest in cashing out. I was making passive income from those investments. Five years later there is another housing market crash coupled with a stock market correction. Business is slow because the economic changes caused layoffs and significant portfolio losses, and potential new clients are too afraid to make any changes until they see the light at the end of the tunnel. I have several obligations between paying employees, taking care of my own expenses, and helping my family, but all of my money is tied up in real estate, and the savings I have that were meant to be put towards another down payment are only enough to sustain me for six months.

I need to sell one of my houses because the rental income alone isn't enough to maintain my lifestyle and fulfill my obligations and one of my tenants just told me she needs to move back in with her parents because she was recently laid off. I meet with a realtor who tells me my home that a few years ago was worth 30 percent more than what I paid for it is now worth 10 percent less than I paid for it and that it'd be nearly impossible to sell the house in the current market without slashing the price by 25 percent of what I bought it for. So I head to the bank knowing that because the appraisal value is high I'll still have some equity I can draw on.

I tell the bank representative that I'd like to open a home equity line. He runs an application with me and tells me that because of my high debt to income ratio and my low net worth (my assets minus my liabilities), they can't offer me a loan. All of those mortgages on my properties—even though they're being paid in full and on time—are actually working against my financial standing. Who would have thought that investing in real estate would have ended up working so strongly against me when I most needed the money?

At that point I only have two options: ride it out and hope at the end of six months I'm back on track financially, or sell one of the houses at a 25 percent loss. Riding it out is too much of a gamble and I know I won't be able to sleep at night with the uncertainty, so I list the house with the biggest spread between what I owe and what I'm being recommended to list it for. In retrospect I wish I had diversified my investments and made sure I had adequate liquidity instead of tying it up in property that wasn't readily convertible to cash. I could have still invested in real estate, but had I spread out my investments I could have held on to my real estate during times when the environment meant it was not ideal to sell and instead cashed out investments that still had value or had less of a loss and were more liquid.

Life happens. When it does, you need to make sure you're able to weather the storms, and lack of diversification—especially in terms of real estate, business investing, and stocks—is dangerous simply because of susceptibility to market changes and lack of liquidity when it comes to your ability to sell.

Every day, I see people leaving their financial lives up to luck or chance instead of taking the steps to add a greater degree of certainty to their plans. I understand why these investments are so appealing: real estate is sexy, stocks are sexy, entrepreneurship is sexy. Why? Because we've heard countless stories of people who have made tons of money these ways through a mix of luck and the ability to spot a good opportunity. We've even experienced success in these areas ourselves, and it's hard to dispute personal experience. Going slow and steady, creating a plan and staying the course, and proper diversification are not sexy, but incorporating those as foundational elements of your financial life means confidence, lower risk, and potentially desirable returns.

True, there are no overnight millionaires created as a result of having a diversified investment portfolio, and there are overnight millionaires who got in on the ground floor and made the decision to purchase Google stock before it exploded. But you know what stories you don't hear? People who continually lose their hard-earned money by taking a gamble on the purchase of a stock like Citigroup, which went from $27.35 on April 28, 2008 to 97 cents seemingly overnight back on April 4, 2009. That was painful if an investor sold at a loss, but for those that could afford to wait it out, it did eventually return to its previous value in May 2010.

On the other hand, if you either needed to cash out or pulled your money out due to fear, you lost 90 percent of your investment. No one talks much about the person who is able to live life on their terms without money stopping them from having their desired lifestyle, but it happens every day for people who plan and are deliberate about implementing these strategies.

> Which areas of your saving lack diversification? Has it hurt you in the past? How are you going to leverage diversification in the future?
>
> Have you felt the need to make rash decisions like selling a stock that tanked based on a change in the environment or based

Lack of planning often creates a false need to "get rich quick." One of my clients tells me all the time that she can't afford not to take chances on picking single risky stocks because she is quickly approaching 70 years old and hasn't done the saving she should have and her health, her sick husband, and her ability to continue working are all huge concerns. That kind of thinking is almost counterintuitive because she can't really afford to lose, either, but I see where it's coming from. One of her stock picks has actually performed exceptionally well, more than doubling her investment in less than a year, but it could have easily gone the other way. Future picks might not fare so well, but we won't know until it happens.

The point is that when you plan, you're less likely to need to make rash decisions or accept losses when timing isn't on your side. Real estate isn't always a great idea, just like investing in the stock market isn't always a bad idea. Both can be exceptional ways to build wealth and optimize your lifestyle, but they need to fit your goals, your risk tolerance, and your financial situation. There is no blanket solution when it comes to investing in any of these areas.

Chapter Questions:

If you're thinking about buying a new home or property, is it for financial/investment reasons or quality-of-life reasons? If financial reasons, how can you determine the actual estimated return, taking risk into consideration, to know if this is really a good investment? If they're quality-of-life reasons, what are you willing to give up to offset this expense so that you are still able to save?

_____

_____

_____

_____

Are you a homeowner who purchased a house as an investment and it turned out not to be? What would you do differently next time? Or if it turned out to be a great investment, how do you know it's a great investment—by running the numbers or some other way?

_____

_____

_____

_____

Have you decided to invest in real estate in the past, or is it something you've been thinking about lately? Why or why not? What would you want it to provide for you or what has it provided already?

_____

_____

_____

_____

When it comes to investing, in real estate or otherwise, do you find yourself more comfortable sticking to one kind of investment that you've had success with in the past rather than diversifying? Why? What intimidates you about diversifying?

_____

_____

_____

_____

Have you ever felt that there is a compelling reason for you to keep all of your eggs in one basket despite being cautioned on the risk? That the answer is so obvious because it has served you so well before? In what area are you not diversifying, and what are you doing elsewhere in your life to minimize the risk this brings? If nothing, pick a way to diversify to add a layer of risk management and write it here.

_____

_____

_____

_____

Have you felt the need to make rash decisions like selling a stock that tanked based on a change in the environment or based on life changes? What were they? Did these decisions set you back financially? If so, what are you doing to prevent a repeat of this?

_____

_____

_____

_____

Which areas of your saving lack diversification? Has it hurt you in the past? How are you going to leverage diversification in the future?

_____

_____

_____

_____

CHAPTER 7

The Entrepreneurship Trap

"Your time is limited, so don't waste it living someone else's life. Don't be trapped by dogma—which is living with the results of other people's thinking. Don't let the noise of other's opinions drown out your own inner voice. And most important, have the courage to follow your heart and intuition. They somehow already know what you truly want to become. Everything else is secondary."
—Steve Jobs

We all know the story of the self-made millionaire entrepreneur. He dropped out of school to pursue a crazy vision that no one else ever thought possible and now, because of the risks he took and his ability to see potential where no one else did, he is living the dream. Money. Prestige. Success by the standards of many. But what about the story of the typical entrepreneur? The one who built a business out of passion or a hobby or simply out of a need to make money? What makes either one of these individuals different from a traditional employee who works for someone else for a paycheck?

Almost everything.

Millionaire or not, those who decide to start their own businesses and find success as entrepreneurs are wired differently than the rest of the population. The environment has changed and entrepreneurship is at an all-time high, with 13 percent of Americans starting or running new businesses. Entrepreneurship is sexy, but as every entrepreneur will tell you, it's hard work to build and maintain a successful business, regardless of the field. Instead of going to the office, getting work done, and going home, entrepreneurs take their work home with them at least mentally, if not physically.

> If you're thinking about starting a business or starting another business, is the desire to do this money driven or lifestyle driven? If it's money driven, have you truly calculated the time and energy that will be required to be both boss and employee, and have you explored all avenues to see whether that income potential is possible as an employee? If it's ifestyle driven, have you accounted for the fact that in order to have a successful business you'll likely need to be prepared to not have that lifestyle for at least the first year and maybe more, because of time and money commitments to your business?

There are so many things wrong with the way both the general public and modern-day entrepreneurs look at entrepreneurship. First, we'll tackle how the everyday employee looks at starting a business. Research done by UPS says that as many as 48 percent of Americans dream of starting a business. Some are actually in the process of getting started, others won't start until months or years have passed, and still others never will make those dreams a reality. What I've learned is that the public perception of entrepreneurship is very skewed and many people get into business very unaware of what they're in for.

Many people thinking about starting a business are drawn in by the prospect of more money, more freedom, and more independence. They figure that instead of being restricted to making how much someone else thinks they're worth via a salary, they can work just as hard and make the same money or significantly more with the same level of effort. They also think that now they can work when they want to, how they want to, and with whom they want to, and they can have complete flexibility in their schedules. While these things are all true in theory, in reality they rarely play out.

As a business owner, you play every role. Instead of working 40 hours as a computer programmer at your job for another company, if you're lucky you work 40 hours as a self-employed programmer and then spend as many other hours as it takes—potentially another 20–40—trying to get clients to hire you for your programming, chasing down money from said clients, updating client files and records, and the list goes on. Unless, of course, you hire people to handle sales, accounting, and administration, in which case you now have salaries to pay. Ideally, these people will be competent and productive and be paid less than what you make per hour programming so you'll get a return on investment there, but you also need to factor in that you now have people to manage and hire and fire. And, if business gets slow, you're still responsible for putting food on your employees' tables.

> Delegating in life is just as important as delegating in business. Time is your most valuable resource. Where are you creating leverage by delegating things in your life and your business?

If you don't hire anyone and stay a one-man show, as many entrepreneurs do, it is extremely hard to grow; you basically cap your income potential because now your $100+ per hour talents are being spent on $10 and $20 per hour work. It's a conundrum because it becomes a case of the chicken and the egg. You need to delegate responsibilities and hire people in order to be more productive, make more money, and do what you truly love, but you need more clients so you have money to hire, which means more time spent building relationships and selling in order to hire anyone. Even when you decide you absolutely need to hire someone, we all know how the saying goes, "Good help is hard to find"—and, you might add, expensive to keep.

The same way entrepreneurs find it hard to delegate in business, many of us find it hard to delegate in life. We'll spend an entire Saturday cleaning the house instead of hiring a professional to clean much faster and do a better job so we can spend more time with our families. Sometimes delegation is a money-saving strategy (pay someone less than you make in order to help you make more), and sometimes it's a time-saving strategy (pay someone to do something in order to earn back valuable time of your own that is better spent or more enjoyable spent doing something else).

We just focused on the money part, but all of that easily applies to the freedom and independence piece as well. In theory, as an entrepreneur you are absolutely free to do what you want with your time, but running a business takes time and energy and both hard work and smart work. Although you can do whatever you want with your time, if you don't spend it working a lot, at least in the first several years, you will likely find it hard to feed yourself and your family and to gain momentum in the marketplace. As a result, entrepreneurs are almost always working or thinking about working, whether they are in the early stages and need to or they are in the later stages and want to grow rather than just plateauing and maintaining the status quo.

> Looking back on your initial reasons for wanting to start a business, do you still think it's the right choice? If you are currently an entrepreneur, have you experienced any of the situations I've described? How have you, or can you, overcome these circumstances to grow your business?

Starting a business is daunting. Many know there is risk involved, and even if they don't fully understand how much risk is associated with being in complete control of their income, they still want a piece of the pie. Maybe their goal is just to earn a little extra income that might buy them a little more freedom through having money to travel or pursue other interests. And here's where many get drawn into multi-level marketing companies. It's a way to get a business in a box, not have to figure everything out yourself, get some extra income in addition to your salary, and hopefully at some point be able to build it to the point where it replaces your full-time job. Easy, right? Not quite.

You might think that now's the time where I turn around and bash every multi-level marketing company out there, saying they're all "pyramid schemes" or scams and all that other craziness people usually say when multi-level marketing comes up in conversation, but it's not. I actually strongly believe that this kind of venture provides great opportunities for people to be their own bosses and get a taste of entrepreneurship, and I know several friends and colleagues who have been involved in different companies and made some pretty decent income from their efforts. But so many people sell these opportunities by saying how easy and low commitment they are—"You can make $1,000 extra per month working only a few hours per week"—and it's simply not true. There is no way you are going to spend just two or three hours of your time per week and make between $80 and $125 per hour. If it were true, everyone would be doing it, likely full time, and it would replace all the $30 per hour jobs out there. If it were true, you'd be a fool not to do it.

> Have you ever joined a multi-level marketing company with the goal of generating some passive income? What was your experience? If it didn't work, why do you think that is?

A multi-level marketing company is a business. It is a simple business in that it's not complicated because the product is there, the strategy is there, and the roadmap to build it is there, but it is not an easy business. In fact, realtors, financial advisors, insurance agents, and mortgage brokers all operate on a similar model and those businesses are just as simple, but definitely not easy. No business is easy. Being in business is inherently hard. It involves failure and rejection and getting up eight times when you fall down seven. I've seen many people mistakenly get into businesses like these because they seem like a no-brainer. Anyone can do it. Yes, anyone can do it. It's not hard to sell a product you like. For some people, it's not even hard to sell a product you don't like. What's hard is finding people to sell it to and getting through the nos to get to the yeses, both with clients and with recruits. Similar to every other business, it's hard work and it takes time to build momentum and a presence in the market. At the core, every business is about relationships, and multi-level marketing is no different.

I've had several clients decide to join different MLM companies and I always tell them the same thing: "It's a business designed to help you make money in two ways, selling product and building a team. Both channels are separate income streams and you really need both to earn great money. You also need to treat it like you own your own business, or you might as well get a part-time job with a paycheck." Many people sign up thinking they are going to ask a few people to buy their product and the money will come rolling in. When it doesn't and when a few people say no, they give up and say it doesn't work, that it's a scam and no one makes money doing it. That makes me so frustrated. I could go open up a convenience store tomorrow and for whatever reason go out of business a year from now, but that doesn't mean convenience stores are a bad business or that they are a scam. There's many a convenience store owner who has made their living from their store and built wealth, likewise with multi-level marketing.

> How do you feel about debt? Do you think this view has helped or hindered your success?

So that being said, if you're part of the 48 percent of Americans who have dreamed of owning their own business, go for it. Whether you design it based on your passion or whether you buy a business in a box, just make sure you love what you're doing, that you are making an impact, and that you are committed to making it happen no matter how hard it gets, because life as an entrepreneur is not for everyone and even those like me—who couldn't picture life any other way—get tired sometimes and want to give up.

For those of you who are entrepreneurs already, there is a lot of conventional wisdom out there that is highly detrimental to your success. Some of it is widely shared and repeated; some of it is the lies we may tell ourselves and don't always share with others. The main piece of conventional wisdom to watch out for is regarding debt, namely that debt is bad.

An entrepreneur's personal beliefs about debt can hinder or skyrocket business growth. Many entrepreneurs, especially sole proprietors who run service-based businesses, buy into this "debt is bad" notion. The entrepreneur who used a business loan to buy a 7-11 isn't going to think debt is bad because without it, he wouldn't have been able to generate the revenues and enjoy the income his store provides—yet the realtor who doesn't have much overhead and works out of his house might look at debt as something to be ashamed of.

It's funny that we look at all debt aside from mortgage and student loans as bad debt, when debt can't really be generally classified by category. The credit bureaus choose to view mortgage debt and student loans as "good debt" and it generally helps your score (or at least won't hurt it), while other debt like car loans and credit card debt is generally looked at as "bad debt" and only helps your credit score in terms of establishing payment history or if cards have low balances.

Our society has internalized these rules of thumb without ever questioning the logic or doing any deeper digging, and it's really worth taking a closer look. Generally speaking, we can further break down good debt and bad debt into two categories: "debt that will make you money" and "debt that will only cost you money." If you follow the conventional wisdom that a home is always a good investment, then a mortgage is always good debt. Likewise, if you follow the conventional wisdom that someone with a college education always makes significantly more money than someone who doesn't go to college, student loans are always good debt also. But what happens if you buy the biggest house on the block (or the house you likely won't be able to sell for much more than you bought it for) or you earn a pricey degree without a plan for how to leverage it for employment opportunities? Is the debt you take on in those cases good or bad? I'd venture to say it's bad.

All debt that has an interest rate greater than 0 percent costs you money, whether it is debt from a mortgage, a student loan, or a credit card. The only "free money" is on a 0 percent interest credit card if you pay it off in full during the interest-free period or an interest-free loan from a friend or family member. Just like you expect to pay interest on a mortgage, fees related to investing in the stock market, or interest on a business loan or on operating expenses, there is a fee associated with borrowing money on a credit card. It is only worth bearing the cost of fees and interest associated with debt or an investment if, after careful analysis, we find there is a way to create leverage and get a return on that investment. Without the leverage that comes in the form of some kind of financing, a loan, or a credit card, we wouldn't have the resources to make an investment that had the power to generate those returns.

I'd say that stretching yourself to pay off credit card debt that built up because of lavish vacations is just as "bad" as stretching yourself to pay the mortgage on a house that is likely to only cost you and never make you money. But making an investment on a credit card—if that's the best means available to you and you have done the analysis or research to know it will create leverage in your life or business—is a no-brainer for me. Many people don't understand how to effectively run a successful business, just like many people don't know how to effectively manage their money. An investment in the advice or tools you need, through a coach, advisor, or certification, could be the difference between earning $10,000 per year and $100,000 per year or even $1,000,000 per year. I'd happily put those costs on a credit card with even 20 percent interest if there was a strong likelihood that this investment would yield me a 200 percent return over time. An investment of this kind, even if put on a credit card, is good debt in my book because it's debt that has allowed you to create leverage and generate a return on your investment.

> Have you been holding off on investing in your business or your financial future because you've been waiting for things to turn around? How long have you been waiting? Has waiting cost you in the long run?

So the previous examples show debt that will simply cost you money while offering no return on investment ("bad debt") and also debt that will make you money and give a return on your investment ("good debt"). I have absolutely no problem telling someone making a good income but in severe debt or with no assets that they should pay a fee for objective financial advice. If you make enough money that Social Security and a small amount of savings just won't cut it in retirement, or that your kids aren't going to easily qualify for need-based financial aid, you make enough money to pay for objective advice. And as you've seen in prior chapters, if you're not paying for advice, the results could be costly. Good financial advice is an investment in your financial future and should help you get the education and tools you need to change your financial habits. To say you shouldn't pay for help until you turn things around (when you likely never will) is like saying don't invest in your business until your business is successful—that simply doesn't work.

You've heard the old adage "It takes money to make money," and in general I think that this piece of conventional wisdom is true, but I'd add "if it's invested in the right places." Sometimes, people use that saying as an excuse to make bad money decisions or gamble, but I'm talking about strategically using money as a tool to make more money. This holds true in traditional stock market investing and it absolutely holds true when it comes to investing in your business.

Many entrepreneurs spend money on all kinds of crazy things that don't make our businesses more money, but we think it's okay because they're "business expenses." I know there are absolutely non-negotiable costs associated with doing business, and I know there are other marketing costs that are negotiable but absolutely necessary because those expenses make you more money than the expense. Smart investments are those things that cost your business money but that you know for a fact—either because of experience or the credibility of what you're investing in—will make you more than what you invested now or plant a seed to help your business grow later.

I firmly believe that you can and should put those expenses on a credit card if you are confident that you will make the money back in a specified period of time. That's right; I am telling you it's okay to take on credit card debt for a business investment if you can say confidently that in a certain number of months you will be able to pay it off. As long as there is actually a plan behind it, I look at the credit card in this case the same as I'd look at a business loan, and I would place it on the same level as investment in a college education that is designed to get you a higher income.

Unfortunately, I often see my clients who own small businesses taking on credit card debt or unable to save because they're putting all the different categories of business expenses into the same bucket. Their car is a business expense. Because it's not directly coming out of the money they're paying themselves they buy the brand-new BMW instead of the used one or instead of the Toyota. They're spending money on fun trips and gifts for their employees that then become regular expenses because it becomes part of the culture, but employee productivity and employee retention aren't going up or correlated at all to the spending. Those kinds of bad money habits and a lack of strategic spending with regard to your business are extremely detrimental because that money could be better spent, either on an investment that makes the business more money or by being put towards your personal financial goals.

The failure to properly invest in education and opportunities for their businesses is what keeps many entrepreneurs working harder than they ever did in corporate America, but also making less money per hour for all of their hard work. Many entrepreneurs could simply go get a full-time job and a part-time job, work the same 60–80 hours per week they're working now, and make more money than they're making in their business—with less stress. It's unfortunate because in many ways these businesses are the lifeblood of our economy and the business owners should be rewarded for the risks they took, but instead they're stuck merely staying afloat, just getting by.

> As an entrepreneur, are you passing up investment opportunities because there is no strategy to your business spending and cash flow is suffering? Is this getting in the way of experiencing the entrepreneurial life you envisioned? What kind of investments would you have made or would you make now if cash flow weren't an issue?

It's another Catch-22 situation. You need to spend money to make money, and many entrepreneurs are afraid to take on debt because they've made "investments" in their businesses in the past and were left worse off than before, with less money and nothing to show for it. For some, the only path to more money and a better lifestyle is to take a risk and invest their last dollars into a strategic investment that gets them the opportunity to reach more clients or higher-quality clients. But to be able to take on this risk without having it completely devastate their entire financial situation, they need to make an accurate assessment of themselves and their situation. Not only do they need the right opportunity, but they need to be committed to make it work no matter what—and the honest truth is that some will spend their last dime or get into debt and they still won't take the steps they know it takes to see the return on investment. I've seen it several times and it's terrifying, but I've also seen lives changed when someone who has no other choice and refuses to take no for an answer takes the risk against all odds.

Another entrepreneurship trap is bad planning, which means we end up playing catch-up—with taxes, with savings, with expenses—and it seems like we never build substantial wealth outside of hard assets like real estate and retirement accounts. The risk of having only illiquid assets such as business, real estate, and retirement accounts when you're pre-retirement age is that when money is tight or something happens, you won't have easy access to cash to cover your expenses. Instead, you'll be forced to either improperly use credit cards to maintain your standard of living, cash out investments that make you money, or pay interest, penalties, or fees to tap into other accounts. Then when a good month comes around you're in catch-up mode and some of that income needs to be used to pay the costs generated in the leaner months. Instead of being able to either save or enjoy that extra revenue, a chunk of it is being paid to institutions or put back into investments at a less-than-ideal time if the market has changed in the meantime. Plus, if you had to cash out investments there was likely a tax cost associated as well.

Don't get me wrong. I love entrepreneurship, and I know that if you do it right, it can provide a level of freedom and lifestyle that I don't believe being an employee can afford you—but it isn't without a cost. I've seen both sides of the unsuccessful-entrepreneur coin: people who dabble in entrepreneurship and are never all in so they waste a lot of time and money and don't have much to show for it, and people who do put in the blood, sweat, and tears but never truly build wealth because they don't plan well in their business, which in turn makes planning for their personal finances a much bigger obstacle.

The fact of the matter is that being in business for yourself means you have so much more on your plate, and sometimes setting up the insurance and investment plans that would be a no-brainer to enroll in as an employee ends up being another to-do item that never gets done. On top of that, paying for insurance and investing seems like just another expense for the self-employed (and not a high-priority one at that), which is a shame and a dangerous place. Although overall the average income for self-employed individuals is surprisingly low, successful entrepreneurs typically out earn their employee peers but don't have much to show for that success and bigger paycheck. Don't let this happen to you!

Chapter Questions:

If you're thinking about starting a business or starting another business, is the desire to do this money driven or lifestyle driven? If it's money driven, have you truly calculated the time and energy that will be required to be both boss and employee, and have you explored all avenues to see whether that income potential is possible as an employee? If it's lifestyle driven, have you accounted for the fact that in order to have a successful business you'll likely need to be prepared to not have that lifestyle for at least the first year and maybe more, because of time and money commitments to your business?

_____

_____

_____

_____

Delegating in life is just as important as delegating in business. Time is your most valuable resource. Where are you creating leverage by delegating things in your life and your business?

_____

_____

_____

_____

Looking back on your initial reasons for wanting to start a business, do you still think it's the right choice? If you are currently an entrepreneur, have you experienced any of the situations I've described? How have you, or can you, overcome these circumstances to grow your business?

_____

_____

_____

_____

Have you ever joined a multi-level marketing company with the goal of generating some passive income? What was your experience? If it didn't work, why do you think that is?

_____

_____

_____

_____

How do you feel about debt? Do you think this view has helped or hindered your success?

_____

_____

_____

_____

Have you been holding off on investing in your business or your financial future because you've been waiting for things to turn around? How long have you been waiting? Has waiting cost you in the long run?

_____

_____

_____

_____

As an entrepreneur, are you passing up investment opportunities because there is no strategy to your business spending and cash flow is suffering? Is this getting in the way of experiencing the entrepreneurial life you envisioned? What kind of investments would you have made or would you make now if cash flow weren't an issue?

_____

_____

_____

_____

CHAPTER 8

Stop Living in Denial

"It's not denial. I'm just selective about the reality I accept."
—Bill Watterson

You've seen them a million times: People who consistently say one thing and do another. A friend who says they're there if you need anything and never answers the phone when you call. A significant other who says they're listening to you and then does the complete opposite of what you asked. A neighbor who constantly complains about their job but never makes any effort to find something else. In all of these situations, I believe that these people do think that what they're saying is true.

But we all know that actions speak louder than words. Research indicates that 55 percent of communication is body language, 38 percent is the tone of voice, and 7 percent is the actual words spoken[12]. So more than half of what you're telling people and what they're telling you is non-verbal, through physical actions. So when you say you love your family, I believe that you mean it, but your actions—the way you save and handle your finances—say otherwise.

Whether you're single or have a family of your own, the way you save and spend impacts those you love. If you don't love anyone, it only impacts you. But we don't live in isolation; we live in communities. We have friends, neighbors, family members; people we share life with who

---

12 "Decoding of inconsistent communications." MEHRABIAN, ALBERT; WIENER, MORTON. Journal of Personality and Social Psychology, Vol. 6(1), May 1967, 109-114. http://dx.doi.org/10.1037/h0024532

we care about and who care about us. When someone loses a family member, gets diagnosed with cancer, gets in an accident, or life gets hard and they just need help, it's the people closest to them who make most of the sacrifice to do what they can to help, either with time or money. Failure to plan makes it that much more likely that at some point you will need help, and that people who care about you will need to make sacrifices that impact their own lifestyles or their own families to help you.

I think education is important, and when I have kids I intend to help them with education throughout their lives and do the best I can. If I sent my kids to public school and made them take out student loans for college, they'd probably turn out fine, but I'd be sending the message through my spending choices that other things that I spent my money on took priority over their education, and that wouldn't be in alignment with my values.

My parents placed a huge emphasis on education and showed it in many ways. Before I was even in elementary school I remember my mom always doing "school stuff" with me. We'd do workbooks on math and grammar and would read constantly. Growing up I always had a book in my hands and because she made it fun, I've always thought homework and exercises were fun and I did them. All of my siblings did too. It took time for my mom to work with us like that instead of sitting us in front of the TV or telling us to go play outside (believe me, we did plenty of that too). I never went to private elementary or high school and I ended up getting into several excellent universities and graduated close to the top of my class with a 3.97 GPA, then went on to accomplish what I've accomplished so far. My parents did help foot the bill for my higher education, and I'm happy to say that because I was able to graduate with no student loan debt (by working all through college in addition to my parents' help), my personal and professional decisions aren't based on the need to pay off a mortgage-sized student loan debt.

I understand that you don't need to spend money to show you value education or to show your kids you love them, but higher education is almost a non-negotiable today, and if the only way you support your kids' education is through lessons as they grow up, I believe you're falling very short of your overall mission as a parent.

I remember reading a newspaper article a few years ago that struck me hard because it hit so close to home. The article was about two young children, whose mom died of a brain tumor. Three months later, their father suddenly died of a heart attack. Most of the article was about what great people the couple were, how much they loved their kids, and what a shame it was that their kids would never know such amazing parents. There was also quite a bit of money talk. According to the article, after his wife died the kids' dad created a crowdfunding page to raise money for his son and daughter's education now that their mom was gone.

Do you know what that tells me? At 39 years old, a woman with two kids who was a vice president at a corporate bank and her husband who worked at a bank as well didn't have the foresight to get life insurance to protect their family. A large piece of the foundation of a solid plan—the protection planning—was completely overlooked by a smart, loving dad and a smart, loving mom who was in perfect health until about six months before she passed away. The day the article was published in the paper, after word had spread to friends and family that the father was gone too, the donations in that higher education fund had reached $83,000. That was over a year ago. Now, the donations are up to $195,962. More than 2,300 friends and strangers donated an average of $85 each to help send someone else's kids to college.

I love that the people who donated rallied together to help a good cause, but I strongly feel that they shouldn't have had to. Upon reading the story, I wasn't sure if at some point in the nine months between his wife getting sick and his own passing the father had purchased life insurance. I hoped he did, since there was no mention of raising money for ongoing support for the son and daughter, only college. About six months later I saw another article about the family. The kids' uncle was doing a fundraiser to tackle the financial aspect of the tragedy and to support the kids. I'm not sure how much they were able to raise through this event, but I know the costs associated with raising someone else's kids is more than financial. I also know that there's a good chance that the money raised for the college fund isn't going to be used for college, unless the family that took in the kids is somehow willing and able to support two young kids financially for the next 15-plus years out of pocket.

Whether the kids are living with grandparents or an aunt and uncle, whoever that caretaker is likely has their own financial goals and challenges that they may or may not have planned for. I'd be willing to bet that if a grandparent suddenly had the responsibility of taking in their two grandkids after losing their children, they'd sacrifice almost anything for those kids, including retirement and any other savings they'd accumulated in order to try to keep some sense of normalcy, and that breaks my heart.

> Has failing to properly plan and have a thorough strategy for your money meant that you've neglected the protection piece of your planning (life, disability, and long-term care insurance)? Why do you think this hasn't been a priority? If you have these benefits through work, can you commit to understanding exactly what you have and determining whether it's adequate? Where have you neglected to make sure you and your family are protected, whether you have kids or not? Who will have to suffer and sacrifice financially as well as emotionally if your lack of planning means family and friends need to step in? Are you okay with doing that to them?

I don't know what those kids will remember about their parents—probably many happy memories—but I also know that as they grow up and are struggling with the grief of losing both of their parents and likely also a feeling of not quite belonging or feeling like a burden and having to navigate the financial stresses every family faces but now without their parents, they will have some pangs of wondering why their parents didn't make sure they'd be okay. That's what parents are supposed to do, right? Protect you?

Before we end, it's important to understand that I'm not saying that people who have operated off conventional wisdom or off of the belief that it will all work out eventually aren't intelligent. Anyone who goes along with the conventional wisdom or has procrastinated in the past and whose actions don't line up with their words simply may not have been exposed to the truth. However, once you know the truth, you can no longer claim ignorance as a defense. And now you know the truth.

Now is the time to figure out what has served you in the past when it comes to your money habits and what hasn't. Are you drowning in debt? Are you debt free, but can never seem to find a penny to save? Are you a saver that knows you aren't saving as efficiently or as much as you should be? What has served you and what hasn't? Also, how badly do you want the goals you said are top priority to you? It's time to admit what hasn't worked, congratulate yourself for what has, and create a plan—either with a professional or on your own. Above all, be honest about whether your actions line up with your words and priorities. I know you agree that actions speak louder than words.

So where do you go from here? How can you find someone who can take you to the next level? If you listen to the guidelines given by the pundits and financial writers in the news and magazines, they'll usually tell you to make sure you find a Certified Financial Planner and make sure that the advisor is fee-only, but I think there is different, extremely important criteria when looking for an advisor whom you're expecting to help you achieve your goals and objectives and not just sell you something.

What I've found working in this industry is that it's just like any other industry. Just because someone has managed to get a certification doesn't mean they're actually good at what they do, and just because someone calls herself a financial advisor doesn't mean she's dispensing very much financial advice. It's confusing because the lines are blurred and even when you are ready to plan it's hard to know whom to trust; past personal experiences or the experiences of family members who have invested with someone or hired someone for advice and didn't have a great experience makes it hard to trust someone else.

The confusion is compounded because there are so many conflicts of interest inherent in the industry. Many people who actually go into their bank and have relationships with the people who work there really trust that institution and those relationships and wouldn't think twice about meeting with the financial advisor at the bank, but you can't assume that just because someone is the financial advisor who works for that bank or credit union or is recommended by them that they will actually do financial planning for you or give you objective advice.

Unfortunately, financial advisors who work for banks are usually either commissioned salespeople or salaried plus a commission so that their compensation is tied to sales of financial products. They also often have quotas they need to meet. These commissions and quotas create huge conflicts of interest and have the potential to put you, the client, in a bad financial position. Some banks also have relationships with financial advisors where they refer their customers to the advisor; the advisor doesn't work for the bank, just with the bank as an added value to clients, or sometimes there is a financial arrangement where the banks receive compensation for business referred to the advisor based on sales and asset management, which can be another conflict of interest.

Am I saying that all advisors who work for or with banks are not good advisors? Of course not! My mom found a great advisor at a local bank other than the one where we do our banking. He is extremely thorough and looks at all aspects of a client's plan and often gives advice that doesn't include a sale because it's the right thing to do. He is a great guy and he cares about each client's goals and objectives. He's built a great business and doesn't need to sell every client something just to put food on his table, and because of the trust he builds he is compensated very well for the time he puts in.

When you're looking for an advisor, don't be afraid to ask how they are compensated for the work you are expecting them to do for you. Commissions aren't always bad, just like working with someone who is only compensated by fees isn't always good, but don't be afraid to ask your current or future advisor how they are paid and what the terms of the relationship are.

To do the best you can when selecting an advisor or evaluating your current advisor, you need to be clear about your expectations and ask them what their goals and expectations are in working with you and what results they're anticipating. If their goals are focused on a specific return on your investments, while your goals are broader and you are looking for advice on how to more effectively manage your money overall, you are not going to be happy or you are going to think your advisor is not doing his job because you aren't on the same page.

Something else to point out is that there is a lot of talk about finding a fee-only advisor. "Fee only" can mean fee for service, as in an hourly rate or annual retainer, or it can mean an advisor receives a flat fee for managing your portfolio that is a percentage of the balance. Fee-only advisors are recommended because the advisor receives no commissions on products sold, which takes away many conflicts of interest—the advisor is compensated the same regardless of what is recommended. But I still don't believe that finding a fee-only advisor is always best.

Many fee-only advisors receive as their compensation a flat fee based on a percentage of your investments. However, even though their advice on what stocks, bonds, ETFs, and mutual funds to invest in is technically unbiased because they receive the same amount of compensation whether you buy you buy a hot tech stock or mutual fund, they are biased in that the more of your money they manage, the more money they make. This also means that they get paid the same amount whether they just talk to you about your portfolio returns or they give you an overall plan looking at your budget, tax returns, debt utilization, and overall financial picture and advise you specifically based on your financial goals.

The more work that advisor does for you, the less money per hour they make. This also means that the less money you have managed by them, the less attention you're likely to get. When advisors are compensated by a percentage of assets, if a client has a small portfolio or is just starting to build a portfolio, the advisor isn't being compensated adequately for their time. The client usually ends up getting very little attention and feeling like the small fish in the big pond. In fact, many advisors who charge fees as a percentage of the client's portfolio balance have account minimums, which means they won't even take your account unless you have that minimum amount for them to invest, because it wouldn't be worth their time otherwise.

The other problem that arises then is that if you have, say, $250,000 minimum to invest, that advisor is getting paid $2,500 per year to manage your portfolio and advise you. If another client has $2.5 million to invest, the advisor is making $25,000 per year to manage that portfolio. Here's a little secret: it doesn't take much more effort to manage $2.5 million than it takes to manage $250,000—but it does take effort to keep that $2.5 million client happy.

That client with the bigger portfolio likely has a more complicated financial situation. The advisor may naturally find it worth his time to spend another 40 hours per year helping that client with a roadmap and navigating their finances. Obviously he won't have to do that if the client is only expecting a good return on their investments—which is what many people expect from their advisors instead of expecting full-service planning. However, is it likely that the advisor would be willing to put in an extra 40 hours to help the client with the $250,000 portfolio do the planning she would need to get to $2.5 million or to achieve her financial goals? Probably not. Again, it depends on the person, but that is why it's so important to ask the difficult questions and see what kind of work the advisor is putting in.

It's quite likely that if you have a fee-only advisor but you have a small portfolio you won't get the planning you need. Ask them about that and be willing to pay an hourly rate or annual fee, if necessary, to get the attention you deserve, but also make sure you ask what their expertise is. If it's in true financial planning, and for many of their clients they look at their entire financial situation and help with strategy to help pursue their specific goals and objectives, then great—the overall benefits and returns you will get from working with someone in this way far outweigh any costs, especially in financial mistakes averted. But if that advisor typically does money management and focuses on investments and getting higher returns, you may not want to have them do your planning because they don't have systems in place around that. And although they may have the knowledge to do it, either because they're a CFP or have other certifications, that is not their expertise, experience, or passion.

I think the fairest way to work with an advisor (for both sides) is to pay them an annual fee for advice and planning. This fee compensates them for their time in helping you establish, maintain, and update the roadmap to more efficiently pursue your goals, and it allows them to help you navigate and follow that roadmap, offering accountability and advice. It also takes away the nickel and diming that I feel hourly billing creates, because knowing you will be billed for an appointment or for picking up the phone for advice is a deterrent and defeats the purpose of having an advisor who can be proactive in working for you.

I also do not think commissions are a bad thing. If your advisor recommends an insurance or investment product as part of your financial plan after you've paid a fee for that advice, and you decide to go to the bank or someone else to purchase that product, that person will receive a commission for helping you through the sale, making sure that it is appropriate. I don't think it's wrong or creates a conflict if your advisor is the one who helps you through the sale of that product instead; they are simply getting compensated for additional work associated with selling that product. What I do think creates a problem is when someone is commission only and is offering to give you financial advice. I know from experience that it is an unsustainable model. That person will have to continue selling you products in order to keep getting paid, which creates a conflict, or if they do the right thing and only sell you products if and when appropriate, they are not getting paid when they meet with you to review or when they help you with other aspects of your planning. That person is also forced to take on more and more clients to keep getting paid, which means there is a good chance they won't be able to give you or any of their clients the level of service that planning requires.

At the end of the day, there are many different models and many different types of advisors, and the best you can do is be clear about what you expect, ask the right questions about the services they offer and how they are compensated for what they offer, and ask them if there are any conflicts of interest they see with their model and how they minimize those. Don't be afraid to ask the right questions and to challenge someone's claim that they give financial advice. Not all advisors are the same and not all have your best interests at heart, and sometimes it's they can't because their model isn't set up to give holistic advice. If it isn't, that doesn't make them a bad person, and it doesn't mean they can't help you buy a product that fits, but it does mean you shouldn't hire them to help you with a financial plan.

If there's one thing I've learned, it's that it's never too late to change your story, and that the best time to start is now. This is a marathon, not a sprint. Don't give up hope, and make the commitment that having a plan for your money is just as important as having a plan for your next vacation. You deserve to reap the benefits of having a plan for your money. The small changes you make once you have a clear view of the outcomes will make all the difference in creating a wealthier lifestyle.

In the end, never lose sight of the fact that money is not the end game. Accruing wealth is not the end in itself—it is a tool to help you live a richer and more full life—for you and for your family.

The power of gaining control over your financial life is the freedom you will be afforded elsewhere—the freedom to do what you love, to pursue the dreams you are passionate about, and to create lasting memories with the people in your life who you love. Money can't replace experiences and relationships; it is there to help you build the foundation for what you want your lasting legacy to be.

If you love your family, save like it.

Chapter Questions:

Has failing to properly plan and have a thorough strategy for your money meant that you've neglected the protection piece of your planning (life, disability, and long-term care insurance)? Why do you think this hasn't been a priority? If you have these benefits through work, can you commit to understanding exactly what you have and determining whether it's adequate?

_____

_____

_____

_____

Where have you neglected to make sure you and your family are protected, whether you have kids or not?

_____

_____

_____

_____

Who will have to suffer and sacrifice financially as well as emotionally if your lack of planning means family and friends need to step in? Are you okay with doing that to them?

_____

_____

_____

_____

ABOUT THE AUTHOR

"I've learned over and over that life happens on its own terms, not mine."
-Kate Walsh

Nicole Peterkin is a Certified Financial Planner™ and the owner of Peterkin Financial, where she provides comprehensive financial planning for a flat fee that isn't tied to assets or income in an effort to make financial advice more accessible.

Nicky started her college career at Boston University on a pre-med track with the intention of moving on to med school and ultimately becoming a neo-natal surgeon. After diving into her major coursework, she had the opportunity to spend her final year taking elective courses interested her. Ever the planner, Nicky saw this as an opportunity to create a Plan B. Why not get a business degree, concentrating in finance, just in case after a few years in the medical field she wanted to pursue something different? So she enrolled in the necessary coursework, doubling up where necessary, and secured a paid internship at a corporate bank to round out her schooling and prepare for her future.

Med school never came, as Nicky's dad died suddenly during her senior year of college, which changed everything. Her priorities immediately shifted and a desire to pursue entrepreneurship emerged. Lessons learned in the aftermath of her dad's passing led to a passion for mastering money and personal finance. As a result, Nicky has helped hundreds of people improve their financial situations using practical advice and strategies centered on their individual goals and objectives.

When she's not talking personal finance, Nicky loves to travel, and has recently been to Cambodia, Singapore, Thailand, India, South Africa, Portugal, and Italy. When she's home, she can be found training and fundraising for several charitable organizations through races like the Bike MS: Cape Cod Getaway and the Boston Marathon, trying her hand at new recipes, and spending time with her dogs, Grayson and Mojo.

Please visit Nicky at www.NicolePeterkin.com and www. PeterkinFinancial.com to learn more about her background and interests. Feedback is always appreciated!